Mindful Teacher, Mindful School

Sara Miller McCune founded SAGE Publishing in 1965 to support the dissemination of usable knowledge and educate a global community. SAGE publishes more than 1000 journals and over 800 new books each year, spanning a wide range of subject areas. Our growing selection of library products includes archives, data, case studies and video. SAGE remains majority owned by our founder and after her lifetime will become owned by a charitable trust that secures the company's continued independence.

Los Angeles | London | New Delhi | Singapore | Washington DC | Melbourne

Mindful Teacher, Mindful School

Improving Wellbeing in Teaching & Learning

kevin hawkins

Los Angeles | London | New Delhi
Singapore | Washington DC | Melbourne

Los Angeles | London | New Delhi
Singapore | Washington DC | Melbourne

SAGE Publications Ltd
1 Oliver's Yard
55 City Road
London EC1Y 1SP

SAGE Publications Inc.
2455 Teller Road
Thousand Oaks, California 91320

SAGE Publications India Pvt Ltd
B 1/I 1 Mohan Cooperative Industrial Area
Mathura Road
New Delhi 110 044

SAGE Publications Asia-Pacific Pte Ltd
3 Church Street
#10-04 Samsung Hub
Singapore 049483

Editor: Jude Bowen
Associate editor: George Knowles
Production editor: Nicola Carrier
Copyeditor: Solveig Gardner Servian
Indexer: Silvia Benvenuto
Marketing manager: Dilhara Attygalle
Cover design: Wendy Scott
Typeset by: C&M Digitals (P) Ltd, Chennai, India
Printed by CPI Group (UK) Ltd, Croydon, CR0 4YY

Library of Congress Control Number: 2016961792

British Library Cataloguing in Publication data

A catalogue record for this book is available from
the British Library

ISBN 978-1-5264-0285-1
ISBN 978-1-5264-0286-8 (pbk)

At SAGE we take sustainability seriously. Most of our products are printed in the UK using FSC papers and boards.
When we print overseas we ensure sustainable papers are used as measured by the PREPS grading system.
We undertake an annual audit to monitor our sustainability.

This book is dedicated to
all the teachers I have known and worked with
- and to all those I haven't. Thank you.

'Teachers, keep on teaching,
Till we reach the higher ground.'
- Stevie Wonder

In memory of exemplary educator, William Powell,
1949-2016

Contents

List of Figures

About the Author

Kevin Hawkins has worked with children and adolescents in various contexts for over 30 years as a teacher, school head and social worker, in the UK, Europe and Africa. In London he worked as a counsellor for drug users and as a resettlement worker for homeless young people. He has taught across the age ranges in state schools and in international schools, with a focus on developing the whole child through balancing academic, social and emotional aspects of learning. He was Head of the Arusha Campus of the International School Moshi in Arusha, Tanzania, and for 10 years was Middle School Principal at the International School of Prague in the Czech Republic.

Kevin started teaching mindful awareness to students, teachers and parents in 2008, and in 2012 he co-founded MindWell (www.mindwell-education.com) which supports educational communities in developing wellbeing through mindfulness and social-emotional learning. Kevin works independently as a speaker, consultant and teacher trainer. He has three grown up children and is based in Prague, where he lives with his wife and work partner, Amy Burke.

Preface

I have been fortunate to train with some leading experts in mindfulness but I certainly do not claim to be any kind of mindfulness guru. I am a teacher and school leader who came across something of value in my own life, something that proved to be of great practical benefit, something that feels significant. So significant that I couldn't understand why we weren't already teaching it in schools. Once I had developed my personal experience with mindful awareness, I looked around to see if I could offer training to students, then to teachers and then to parents. This book derives from that journey and I offer it as one educator to other educators; to teachers, support staff, counsellors, psychologists, school leaders and administrators - as well as to interested parents - with the hope that it may bring some clarity and coherence, demystify some commonly held misconceptions about mindfulness in education, and show how it can benefit school communities.

I have a passion about developing mindful awareness and social-emotional skills in schools because I have felt the benefits of this work in my life, and seen it benefit so many others. However, when I say 'mindfulness can do this' or 'it can help us do that', I do not mean to say that it is a panacea. I don't believe it is. It needs to be seen as one element within a range of possibilities such as good exercise, healthy diet and sound sleep that contribute to overall wellbeing. Many people find it helpful, some life-changing. There are though many misperceptions around meditation and mindfulness and sometimes these can put people off even trying. My hope is that this book will encourage you to try things for yourself, with an open mind, and just see.

At the end of each chapter (except the first and last) you will find ideas for further reading and suggestions for things you might want to try out for yourself. There are many practical examples and suggestions, but this book is not a manual or a course - it is more an invitational guide for educators. My hope is that it might open a door for you, invite you in to take a look around, get a feel for it, and then you can decide for yourself if there might be something of value here, for you, your students and your school. If you have already set foot on your own journey, I hope that these words, ideas and experiences will offer validation and support in seeking to shift the focus of our schools towards areas that have for too long been marginalised in mainstream education, and which have the potential to cultivate capacities that the world right now is very much in need of.

Acknowledgements

For their kind permission to use their words, experiences, ideas and images, I am greatly indebted to Tim Burns, David Rock, Richard Burnett, Chris Cullen, Krysten Fort-Catanese, Jason Tait, Jason Pendel, Petr Dimitrov, Solange Lewis, Catherine Ottaviano, Andy Mennick, Richard Brown, Katinka Gøtzsche, Helle Jensen, Ann Maj Nielsen, Peter Senge, Mette Böll, Lucy Hawkins, Katherine Weare, Kathlyn Gray, Amy Saltzman, Meena Srinivasan, Linda Dusenbury, Mark Greenberg, Shui-Fong Lam, Stanley Chan, Emma Naisbett, Amy Footman and Liz Lord.

Almost all of what I know about teaching and learning has come from other teachers and students. I am very grateful to have been able to work with some wonderful educators, counsellors, administrators, students, parents and support staff in Yorkshire (Keighley Upper School, Swire Smith Middle School, Waverley Middle School), in Tanzania (International School Moshi, Arusha Campus - *Hamjambo!*), and at the International School of Prague (especially the middle school teachers and Arnie Bieber). Special thanks also to: Bart Dankaerts, Kili Lay and the teachers of The American School of The Hague; Malcolm Nicolson, Robert Harrison, Lucia Capasso, Phillippa Elliot and Christelle Bazin at the IBO (what a team!); Derek Harwell and all at ELMLE; Cheryl Brown and Brooke Fezler at ISCA.

My thinking about the big picture of education was radically revitalised by meeting John Abbott many years ago. He twice came out to work with my school community in Tanzania - for no fee - and his profound thinking about the history, purpose and potential of education underlies much of this book.

My mindfulness journey has been deeply enriched by opportunities to learn directly from some amazing people and teachers, including Mark Williams, Thich Nhat Hanh, Saki Santorelli, Jon Kabat-Zinn and Chris Cullen. Huge thanks also to the trainers and staff at Mindfulness in Schools Project - especially Claire Kelly, James Gibbs and, of course, Richard Burnett.

Special thanks to Kara Smith for initiating the MindWell journey and for finding Amy. Our MindWell connections have been a rich source of joy and inspiration - thanks to Krysten for being at the heart of it all.

The wonderful Sarah Hennelly checked over the latter drafts (all mistakes are mine) and made many helpful and insightful comments - thank you, Sarah. My meditation companion, comrade in mindfulness operations and good friend Tony Ackerman provided sound feedback on ideas, style and my lack of commas. Thanks to you, and Helena also, for the refuge.

Is it possible to write a book advising others on how to become more calm and mindful and yet still get stressed out yourself? Yes, totally! The mindfulness practice did, to be honest, help me a great deal whilst writing this book, but I also owe a huge debt of gratitude to my co-collaborator, work partner, advisor and indispensable other: my wife, Amy Burke. To say this would never have happened without her is a totally true clichéd understatement. The book is based on work that Amy and I developed together and she has been at my side and contributing from the very first spark of the idea, throughout the entire writing process, to the final late-night edits. She is an awesome editor, always ready to read, review, support and question. Above all, thank you Amy for your good cheer, your love and your care - you have kept me sane!

I am deeply grateful to Jude Bowen, my publisher at SAGE, for her wise advice and her excitement and encouragement from start to finish. It's a much better book because of the direction and feedback she has given me. Thanks to George Knowles for his valuable support, to Nicola Carrier in Production, Dilly Attygalle in Marketing and all the rest of the crew at SAGE. I feel very fortunate to have worked with such a great team for my first book.

Last but not least, it is impossible for me to adequately articulate my deep sense of gratitude to three young people with whom I have had the privilege of sharing a journey of growth and discovery: my amazing children, Lucy, Rosa and Billy. Thank you for your interest and for your encouragement. Especially thank you for everything you have taught me about children, life, learning and love.

May you all be well!

Kevin Hawkins

Praise for the Book

'If there is hope for deep societal change, it surely must rest on rethinking and recreating our industrial-age education system. It is within this context that we need to view the growing interest in mindfulness in schools, which could, potentially, help guide us toward a system of education truly oriented toward human development. But it could also end up as just another in a long line of educational fads. Work like that of Kevin Hawkins – based on the science and practice of cultivating mindfulness and grounded in extensive practical experience in schools – could tell the difference.'

Peter M. Senge, Senior Lecturer in Leadership and Sustainability, Massachusetts Institute of Technology

'This book is written for teachers, by a teacher. Kevin truly understands the joys of teaching and the desire to make a real difference to students' lives, as well as the challenges and risks of burnout that most teachers experience on a daily basis. It provides teachers with the essential skills for self-care that will allow them to thrive in their professional and personal lives. It also offers a straightforward, natural progression: from being mindful, to teaching mindfully and engaging students, to teaching students mindfulness, and finally developing and sustaining a mindful school culture. *Mindful Teacher, Mindful School* is an excellent resource for those who want to begin, or to deepen, their own personal mindfulness practice, and to share their practice with students and the wider school community.'

Amy Saltzman, MD Author of *A Still Quiet Place: A Mindfulness Programme for Teaching Children and Adolescents to Ease Stress and Difficult Emotions* (New Harbinger, 2014)

'Kevin has managed something I haven't seen before in a book aimed at educators – he has combined theory with practice and real life stories and with a credibility borne out of experience. Without doubt, mindfulness will play a huge part in supporting the wellbeing of students and teachers. One of the best ways to incorporate mindfulness in a school is for teachers to experience and model it, before they teach it. Crucially, this book shows how to do exactly that.'

Malcolm Nicolson, Director of Erimus Education; Head of IB MYP Development (2007-2013); Head of IB DP Development (2013-2015)

'In *Mindful Teacher, Mindful School*, Kevin Hawkins presents a rich developmental approach to educating the whole child. This book illustrates how mindfulness can enrich teaching and the lives of teachers and students. But Hawkins also is appropriately cautious in suggesting that teachers take time to develop their own practice and awareness. The book is full of practices that can help teachers and all educators embody mindfulness in their daily life. This is quite a gift!'

Mark T. Greenberg, PhD, Bennett Chair of Prevention Research, Penn State University

'*Mindful Teacher, Mindful School* contains real depth of understanding about this important new mindfulness-based approach to education. Radiating from a central theme of teacher self-care, Kevin Hawkins invites the reader to explore the richness of truly international perspectives on mindful awareness and social emotional learning. In an easily readable and common sense fashion he skilfully weaves together research, practice exercises, educational applications, plus the author's and other teachers' own experiences. A rich and compelling tapestry, *Mindful Teacher, Mindful School* is an essential text.'

Richard C. Brown, Professor of Contemplative Education, Naropa University

'This is an elegant and practical guide to cultivating mindfulness in school. With great clarity, wisdom, and warmth, Kevin Hawkins illuminates the paths for being mindful, teaching mindfully and teaching mindfulness. This book explains both the science and practice of mindfulness in school context. It offers teachers not only helpful resources but also accessible steps towards transforming themselves, their students, and their schools.'

Shui-fong Lam, PhD Professor, Department of Psychology, The University of Hong Kong

'*Mindful Teacher, Mindful School* is an invaluable resource for educators. Through his own experience as a school leader and classroom teacher, Kevin Hawkins offers a comprehensive, inspiring and practical approach that makes mindfulness accessible to anyone working in school based settings. Each chapter beautifully builds on each other and helps us see how mindfulness can be a vehicle for not only transforming education but making the world a better place.'

Meena Srinivasan, MA, NBCT, Author of *Teach, Breathe, Learn: Mindfulness In and Out of the Classroom* (Parallax, 2014) and Programme Manager for the Office of Social and Emotional Learning, Oakland Unified School District

'What really matters in education? This book argues that it is educating the mind and heart, equipping the next generation not only with knowledge, but also with how to think, with qualities of curiosity, compassion, playfulness and resilience. Drawing on his immense repository of teaching experience and with deep humility Kevin Hawkins offers an invaluable toolkit for teachers and schools. Anyone using this toolkit will be standing on the shoulders of a very skilful teacher who embodies what he teaches.'

Willem Kuyken, Professor of Clinical Psychology University of Oxford

'In his new book *Mindful Teacher, Mindful School*, Kevin Hawkins takes us on a compelling personal and universal journey of self discovery that is at the heart of the art and discipline of mindfulness. Through this book, we learn that mindfulness has a rightful place in schools, as a powerful tool to help students learn to live in the present and improve their sense of self-awareness. Through anecdotes from schools around the world and through his own personal journey, Hawkins provides us with a down to earth and accessible approach for teachers and students alike to become more mindful human beings.'

Dr Arnie Bieber, Director, International School of Prague

'This book is indispensable for anyone who truly wants to understand what is involved in bringing mindfulness to K-12 education around the globe. Rather than seeing mindfulness as a set of classroom activities to be inserted into the status quo, Kevin Hawkins makes the case for the power of mindful awareness to be part of a much larger transformation of what and how we teach. Proposing that we broaden the aims of education to include physical, mental and emotional wellbeing, Hawkins situates mindfulness – first for adults and then for students – as a catalytic tool within this larger frame. *Mindful Teacher, Mindful School* not only offers everything that someone new to the field needs to get up to speed but also pinpoints deeply important truths for those of us already active in the field. This is a must read!'

Rona Wilensky, Director of Mindfulness Programmes, PassageWorks Institute

'This is a book clearly written by an educator who knows mindfulness in schools from the inside. The strongest evidence for this is that Hawkins never gets carried away. He recognises that mindfulness is not a panacea, that to implement it successfully in schools is a slow and steady process, and that above all it must begin with the teachers themselves. But Hawkins also recognises how transformative mindfulness can be, having experienced it so profoundly himself as an educator in many different contexts. His anecdotes give it plenty of colour (my favourite is 'Billy and the Mosquito'), whilst the practical guidance – Chapter 7 on implementation for example – makes it of tremendous practical value.'

Richard Burnett, Co-founder and Director, Mindfulness in Schools Project

'This book is *elegant*. For all of us aspiring to be educators it is an enduring reminder of our deep inheritance – what the great 13th century teacher, poet and mystic, Jalaludin Rumi, described as "two kinds of intelligence": *one acquired, the other already complete and preserved inside you.* Surely, both these intelligences are important. With humility and wisdom, Kevin Hawkins, a long-time educator, middle school principal and mindfulness practitioner, helps us *remember* the bounty of the "already completed" and the way in which what is innate informs what is "acquired". With substance and grace, the lineages of education, psychology, and neuroscience converge as Hawkins illuminates the critically important role that mindfulness plays in the education of our children, their teachers, and we, their parents.'

Saki F. Santorelli, EdD, MA, Professor of Medicine, Director, Mindfulness-Based Stress Reduction Clinic (MBSR), University of Massachusetts Medical School

MindWell Weblinks

Visit **http://www.mindwell-education.com**

Kevin Hawkins is co-founder of MindWell Education which offers a global network of best practices and evidence-based approaches to social and emotional learning and mindfulness.

The MindWell website also includes a dedicated page for *Mindful Teacher, Mindful School* which includes access to all weblinks within this book.

1

Shifting the Focus

Education today is so pressured, so overstuffed, that every now and then we need to strip away all the clutter and come back to basics. To try to simplify things. One question I sometimes pose to students and teachers at the start of the school year is:

> 'We're actually just a bunch of kids and a bunch of adults, in a building; so really the question is, "How are we best going to spend our time together"?'

This kind of focusing question can be helpful when trying to look at the big picture, develop curricula or explore behavioural norms. In order to answer this question, as educators and as parents, we need to ask ourselves another:

> 'What really matters?'

Given the competing demands on school programmes, this question can help us explore the role and purpose of schools on a deeper level. With overcrowded curricula and overly busy school days we need to learn to let go of things, not continually keep adding on. We can't do it all. So we need to be clear about what really matters.

Ask yourself now, as a parent, thinking of your own children, or as an educator, thinking of the children you teach:

> 'What do you really want for your children?'

Ask yourself again - don't rush to answer this - take a moment, take a breath and allow a response to emerge:

> 'What do you really, deeply, want for your children?'

Make a note of your top three words or phrases before reading further.

When we ask this question of parents and teachers in workshops, these are the type of answers we get:

Self-esteem	Ability to make good decisions
Compassion	Curiosity
Happiness	Imagination
Excitement	Joy
Wellbeing	Resilience
Fulfillment	Well-equipped to deal with life
Self-belief	

Occasionally a parent (or teacher) may say 'Hard-working' or 'Successful' but these more traditionally expressed objectives of schooling are very much in the minority. Although the type of responses listed above may connect quite well to the glossy mission statements of many progressive schools, how often do they align with our students' daily experiences of life in a learning organisation?

There is so much more to effective human learning than grasping at concepts and regurgitating content. The importance of explicitly acknowledging these deeper qualities – for making more space for inner life and for the experience of the learner – will be a core theme of this book. When we *do* give these areas more focus in our schools and in our lives, we can also achieve more. Learning how to deepen our attention, and to become more self-aware, can enhance our academic capacities and make learning more relevant and more impactful.

So, our essential, guiding question is:

> 'Can we begin to shift schooling to more effectively meet these fundamental needs for growth and development?'

Our intention as teachers does not need to start with changing the whole system – much of this book is about how we can first start to shift the focus within ourselves before seeking to change the rest of the world. Indeed, this is the only shift that can make a real difference, and as we learn to draw on a wider and deeper range of our own capacities, we will naturally begin to help shift the focus in our students and in our schools.

THE FORGOTTEN TAXONOMIES

Bloom's Taxonomy of learning (Bloom et al., 1956) was created in the 1950s to help teachers and schools formulate a framework for the key skills to be developed through education. Many teachers have been brought up on Bloom's Taxonomy and almost all have been influenced by it – whether we know it or not. Even if it wasn't explicitly on the agenda during your training, it will probably have informed the teachers who taught you and the educational system in which you operate. It may well have had an indirect impact on your deeper assumptions about learning.

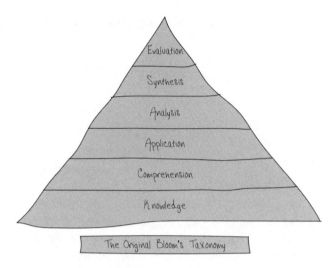

Figure 1.1 Bloom's Taxonomy – Cognitive Domain

What many people don't know though, is that the taxonomy we are familiar with is just *one of three* that were drawn up by Bloom's committee at the time. The one we all know is the taxonomy of **Cognitive** development – dealing with *Knowledge, Comprehension, Application, Analysis, Synthesis and Evaluation.* Somehow the other two – **Psychomotor** (physical) skills and **Affective** (emotional) skills – have been largely forgotten.

Why have we forgotten these two taxonomies? It's not an accident; it's sympto-matic of educational approaches that fail to aim to develop the whole child. Many schools these days do place an emphasis on physical activities and many have

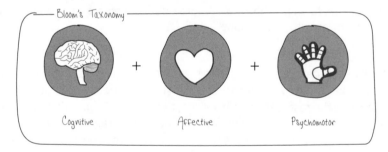

Figure 1.2 Bloom's Taxonomy – Domains of Learning

begun to incorporate elements of social and emotional learning (SEL) into their programmes. But overall, we are a long way from giving young people an expe-rience of schooling that helps them develop into well-rounded individuals with a balanced focus on body, heart and mind.

FINDING BALANCE

The underlying concern that drives this book is: the world is out of balance:

- There are serious questions about our collective mental health.
- As a species we are very clever but we lack wisdom.
- Many education systems both reflect and perpetuate this imbalance.

There is a fundamental problem with our ability to live well and to be well – to share this planet in harmonious ways and to make wise choices about our actions.

This imbalance in human development and activity shows up in so many ways. Our technological prowess is extraordinary. Measuring devices have recently been devised to record gravitational waves with instruments so sensitive they can detect changes in the distance between us and the nearest solar system down to the width of a human hair. We are amazingly clever. But cleverness alone is not enough – we are not so clever, or even very knowledgeable, when it comes to sharing the planet sustainably. Powerful technological skills driven by economic incentives that often only benefit a minority, combined with an inability to see the big picture clearly and to make sound decisions about our actions and their impact, create an unhealthy mixture for ourselves, other species and the planet.

Mainstream school systems often reflect this imbalance. Most schools are good at developing certain capacities and approaches – namely the academic, analytical and critical – but not so good at cultivating the collaborative, social and affective skills that can provide this much needed balance of heart and mind. True education involves more than just becoming smarter – it demands that we cultivate *all* our capacities. The Greeks knew this, and as Aristotle said:

> 'Educating the mind without educating the heart is no education at all.'

What we lack is wisdom. We need to balance our heads and our hearts with an embodied wisdom that can help us find the courage to face complex issues and take wise actions that benefit all.

The core intention of this book is to encourage individual educators and schools to begin to *shift the focus* towards a more balanced and more heart-centred environment that can truly tap the full range of human capacities in the young people we work with and want so much for.

In a complex, challenging world, we need our children to develop resilience, self-awareness and the capacity to be able to make sense of complex systems. We can consciously nurture these neglected competencies in our schools.

HOW WELL ARE WE?

In order to be well and to live well, a degree of economic security is clearly essential, but it's only part of the story. Even those of us who are lucky enough to live in economic comfort aren't necessarily getting any happier. The World Health Organization predicts that by 2030 depression will be the single biggest cause of ill health worldwide (WHO, 2012). A 2005 *British Journal of Psychology* paper indicated that half of us in the West will experience depression in our lifetimes (Andrews et al., 2005).

Especially at risk are the elderly and, more recently, the young. We live in a time of crisis for the mental health of young people. Much of the recent growth of interest in wellbeing and mindfulness in schools in the UK is coming less from education and more from public health officials concerned about an epidemic of mental instability amongst young people:

- 1 in 10 of the 5-16-year-olds in the UK now have a diagnosable psychiatric condition (Mental Health Foundation, 2015).

- Globally, depression is the top cause of illness and disability among adolescents, and suicide is the third highest cause of death (WHO, 2016).

The age of onset of clinical depression is getting younger and younger. Just 50 years ago the most common age for the onset of major depression was seen in people in their 40s and 50s; now it's in their 20s. In fact, one study showed that the new peak age for the onset of major depression is amongst 13-15-year-olds (Williams et al., 2012).

Poverty can add a whole other dimension to these psychological factors, but anxiety and depression know no boundaries. Even if you work in privileged private or international schools, you will know that many of our young people are no strangers to the negative impacts of psychological stress.

We don't know exactly why this downward trend in mental health is affecting people at an increasingly early age, but the impact on learning and growth is highly worrying. Education systems that put a lot of focus on high-stakes exams (and I guess that includes most of them) certainly contribute to the stress young people feel. My three children grew up in international schools and all have now taken the International Baccalaureate Diploma. It's a very well regarded pre-university qualification and a well-thought through framework for a well-rounded final two years of school. But in reality I have to say that, much as I respect and admire the overall concept of the programme, in practice it is just far too demanding. Each teacher wants you to do well in their subject and as results are published there is significant pressure on teachers too. This for me is a clear example of how a lot of well-intentioned people and ideas in a complex system can end up having a negative effect on some of the individuals it was intended to serve. The International Baccalaureate Organization (IBO) is aware of these concerns and is looking at ways to reduce stress (Hawley, 2016). Similar issues, of course, arise for students coping with exam stress in the UK (Ali, 2016) and in many other countries. It's part of a bigger picture in which school systems continue to be filtering mechanisms for increasingly competitive university places – and along the way there are many casualties.

In addition, many of our young people today are often sleep deprived – their lives may be dominated by a battery of digital 'weapons of mass distraction'. If you are in your late teens and live in a wealthy country, chances are that you have had a pretty intense connection to a number of screen-based devices for over half your life. As a school leader, I have been responsible for introducing IT programmes and I appreciate the many ways technology has opened up learning for us all. But digital learning brings its own issues of compulsion and distraction, which we now need to equip our students to deal with.

And it's not just the young who are struggling with this – it's teachers, parents, you, me, all of us. We live in an age where *busyness* and being switched on 24/7 are the norm. It's the nature of modern life and we are all more or less becoming dependent on information technology. If, as adults, we know how challenging it can be to manage our own screen time, can we really expect a 10-year-old to know when to pull themselves back from being sucked in?

We can't put all the blame for modern stresses on technology and social media – changes in general in recent times have been enormous. The increased pace of life is one major cause of our experience of stress. There's an interesting analogy in the book *Sapiens: A Brief History of Humankind* (2014) by Yuval Noah Harari: if someone in the year 1000 fell asleep like Rip Van Winkle for 500 years, and woke just as Columbus was setting sail for the Americas, he would be in shock but the world would be recognisable. However, if one of Columbus' sailors fell asleep in 1500 and woke up 500 years later, he wouldn't know what planet he was on. We are not necessarily hardwired to deal with this increased pace of life.

In order to be successful and resilient in this age of distraction and complexity, there are some basic competencies that we have to learn – or perhaps to redis-cover. We need to consciously cultivate our skills of:

- Attention
- Self-awareness
- Emotional regulation

It's not simply that we need to learn these skills in order to be able to cope with all the problems of modern life, it's also that modern life is giving us many insights into human behaviour that we can draw from – about how the brain works and about how humans best learn. We now know much more about the importance of *attention*. We know from studies of taxi drivers (Maguire et al., 2006) and violinists (Elbert et al., 1995) that we can change our brain by the way we use it. *Where* we put our attention and *how* we pay attention are key factors in understanding how to learn effectively.

Our understanding of the brain has improved so much through brain imaging techniques over the last 20 years, and it is helping us see what happens when people consciously work with their minds. One 'big understanding' is about the plasticity of the brain. **Neuroplasticity** helps us understand the value of training and of retraining and significantly expands our vision of human potential. We are also learning more about how we can train affective skills and capacities such as empathy and compassion as well as how to improve our capacity to attend and to use our minds to their fullest potential.

But our definition of intelligence in mainstream schooling is still far too limited. Testing regimes still dominate our approaches to assessing understanding, and this gives confusing messages to children about the deeper purposes of education.

THE FILTERING SYSTEM

When I was 10 years old we were all made to sit a one-hour IQ test. This test filtered those who did well, on that day, in that hour, from those that didn't. Most of my friends didn't. So I went to the posh grammar school with the silly caps and the bright green blazers, whilst most of my friends went to the much tougher secondary modern school down the road, with the dull green jackets (and no caps). The transition was, for me, a regression – from feeling quite mature and valued in my relatively progressive mixed-gender primary school class, to being the youngest and shortest of 800 boys in an antiquated grammar school (not a great place to be when you are 11 years old). The focus was strictly on academic success and I got myself through the 13 'O' level, 3 'A' level and 2 'S' level exams I sat from age 13–17, but there was no joy in it. I learnt to be more critical, more analytical, and there was some satisfaction in the academic success, and of course in getting a place at a university, but I didn't feel I had really grown in the deeper way I had in my primary school years.

On the day I got my final results at university I thought to myself 'Not bad at all, considering I really didn't work that hard for it'. The very moment I had that thought, it suddenly became clear to me for the first time that no one else would really care that much about my result. Useful perhaps for getting me into some lines of work, but really what did anyone care about that particular number? And why did it matter to me anyway what anyone thought? It was, after all, my education, my career, my life. I had been jumping through academic hoops without really understanding why. The possibility that I could have been studying and learning for the pleasure of it or for my own benefit had never really occurred to me.

As I readied myself to finally step away from an education system that had absorbed much of my waking hours for the past 16 years it suddenly felt like it had all been a sort of game – one that I didn't know I had been playing until that moment.

That narrow view of intelligence that saw my friends and me sifted by IQ test results at such a young age no longer holds quite such sway. Education has moved on since then (thank goodness) and many countries no longer base key life decisions on such narrow parameters at such an early age. But it has not moved on enough – the UK government has plans to increase the number of grammar schools as I write, and we are still obsessed with grades and numbers and other extrinsic motivators that take the focus of learning away from an intrinsic sense of discovery and from the joy of learning itself – and we are still confused about whether school is about learning for life or filtering for college.

In terms of rational, scientific understanding of human learning, we know there's so much more to being 'intelligent' than we thought even a few decades ago. We know there are multiple aspects of intelligence, and we know that our IQ is just the tip of the iceberg. A high IQ may help get you a good job, but it's our other capacities – our emotional and interpersonal skills – that can enable us to make something of that job; to build leadership skills, to grow and develop. Many companies know this – some actively recruit and promote for emotional intelligence – but do our schools really reflect these developments?

> Understanding ourselves, our minds, bodies and emotions, is a key 21st-century life skill.

A legitimate function of schools can be to foster this understanding. If we know more about how to use our minds effectively, how to train the attention, how to develop awareness and build emotional regulation, and if we appreciate the value of these key life skills, should they not be more central to our school curricula?

WHAT WE WANT FOR OUR CHILDREN, WE NEED FOR OURSELVES

How can this shift of focus be achieved? The key, of course, lies with you, the teacher.

It is becoming increasingly important to society that we value and develop these self-awareness and self-management capacities in our students, but for this to happen we need teachers who value, and who are developing, those same capacities in themselves; educators who are emotionally and socially intelligent as well as intellectually and academically knowledgeable.

The importance of the role of the teacher is not fully recognised in many societies. Teachers are often undervalued – by parents, schools, governments – and even by themselves.

> The role of the teacher is vital – it is powerful and it needs our attention.

I say this not just because I am a teacher but because of the significant scientific research in this area (particularly in social neuroscience) and also because it aligns with my own experience.

MWALIMU

When I left university in the 1970s I had no idea what I wanted to do with my life, but the one thing I knew for certain was that I didn't want to spend my precious time teaching. I knew too well what terrors we inflicted in those days on some of our teachers at Chichester High School for Boys; the exhaustion, breakdowns and departures from what had promised to be a noble profession.

(Continued)

(Continued)

Over the years I saw too many friends who had chosen to teach getting worn down and cynical.

But the best laid plans of mice and men …

At the age of 30 I found myself wanting to review my career path (I was a social worker in the voluntary sector) and after a period of reflection ended up choosing to move along a 'road more travelled'. One of my prime motivators in deciding to become a middle school teacher in particular was the horrible transition I had experienced as a child in moving from primary to secondary school. Surely there had to be a better way of doing this?

I started my new career as an ESL (English as a Second Language) teacher in upper and middle schools in Bradford, Yorkshire where I encountered some inspirational teachers working in challenging inner-city situations who found meaningful ways to connect with students and to somehow make an overly prescriptive national curriculum schooling relevant to the children they taught. Years later I somehow found myself in East Africa, starting up a very small 'Junior Secondary' school for 9-13-year-olds that was being added on to a growing English language primary school in Arusha, Tanzania.

From the moment I stepped off the plane I, as a teacher, was made to feel respected, honoured and valued. Not just by the small international community the school had been set up to serve, but also in general, because in Tanzania education is highly valued. The then President, Julius Nyerere, had been a schoolteacher himself and his popular nickname was 'Mwalimu' or 'Teacher'. There is such hunger for education in Tanzania that, despite underpaid teachers with very limited resources, and schools that are sometimes literally just the shade of a tree, children often walk proudly for many miles for the chance to become educated. Coming from the somewhat cynical staffrooms of some pretty tough schools in Thatcherite Britain, where the government almost seemed to despise, and certainly to mistrust teachers, and where parents in our communities could sometimes appear indifferent to the importance of education, this experience of automatically being respected was unsettling – in fact, slightly spooky.

To have a parent community that openly supports, respects and values its teachers is a real gift to a school. Starting that school in an old bungalow in Arusha with just 30 children, one set of atlases, one set of dictionaries and one unreliable computer was one of the best experiences of my teaching career. Strip away all the clutter and it was so obvious to us as a small group of teachers that the essential elements of a school are the students, the teachers and the parents – and the quality of the relationships that connect them.

The central aims of this book are:

- To help shift the focus of mainstream schooling to incorporate more centrally the often overlooked affective capacities that are increasingly understood to be core, not fringe elements, in a school that truly aims to meet the needs of the 21st century.

- To help teachers and schools consider the benefits of using mindful awareness training as a basis for developing these skills within an integrated framework that promotes wellbeing in their communities.

- To help individual teachers – and especially young teachers and trainee teachers – to be able to deeply value the importance of their role, and to help them discover practical ways to sustain themselves and to thrive in this exacting and rewarding profession.

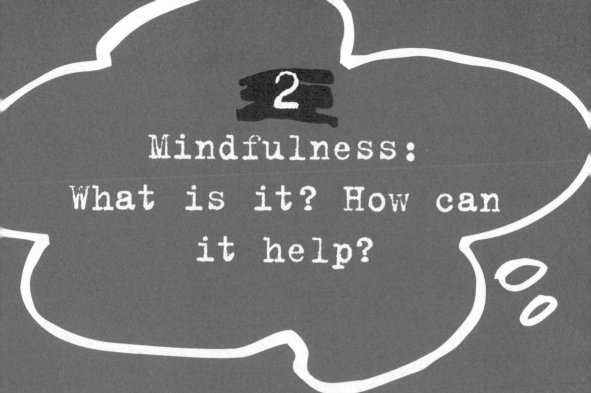

2

Mindfulness:
What is it? How can
it help?

This chapter:

⤳ explores the nature of mindfulness, particularly in its modern context

⤳ looks at how mindful awareness training can help us move from 'thinking mode' to 'sensing mode', opening up possibilities for greater choice about how we respond in various situations

⤳ considers how mindfulness is being used to help with pain, stress, anxiety and depression.

'YOU ARE A YOUNG MAN IN INDIA AND YOU ARE THINKING TOO MUCH.'

This much I knew already, but to hear it coming from the mouth of a turbaned fortune-teller on the Bombay dockside seemed to give it a legitimacy that worried me even further. 'I know I think too much. But how do I stop?' That is what I didn't understand. Trying *not* to think wasn't working.

In the 1970s, whilst on a trip to India I ended up, by chance, taking part in a few meditation sessions with some local people in Pondicherry. This experience had a strong impact on me and I continued to explore meditation when I returned to London. Although I persisted through much of my life to practice yoga or Tai Chi, my meditation practice was very sporadic. Then, during a very difficult period in midlife, when death and divorce created challenges I felt ill-equipped to face, I rediscovered meditation and mindfulness.

I found myself once again journeying down some of those avenues towards self-awareness that I had explored in my youth. In doing so I developed some essential skills and capacities that really helped me to deal with these major life events and to cope better with managing the stresses of life, work and family at that time.

I had to learn how to allow and process strong emotions such as sadness, anger, guilt and grief and as I did so I began to notice, and then gradually to let go of, some self-created stressors. Those subtle, under-the-surface 'stories' about my difficulties that were only making things worse. I began to discover for myself the value of what it means to really be consciously present, even in the midst of difficulty. And beyond this, to sense a capacity for enjoying life more fully again.

Thus, decades later, the introduction to meditation I had received in my youth proved to be a highly significant experience for me. After I had established my own daily practice and done some further training, an obvious next step seemed to be to introduce students, teachers and parents to mindfulness. In subsequent chapters we will look in depth at how this can be done in schools, but first we will focus directly on what mindfulness is, where it comes from and how it can help.

FIFTEEN SECONDS

In the 1960s, a wave of 'seekers' (the trailblazers for my own overland trip in the following decade) travelled from the West out to Asia. It was the encounters of some of those individuals with Eastern practices that laid the foundations for some valuable, cross-cultural learning that has resonated down the decades into the present day, and into mainstream science, psychology and medicine. In 1979, Jon Kabat-Zinn, a molecular biologist at Massachusetts Institute of Technology, USA, was sitting in a meditation group in Barre, Massachusetts, when he had 15 seconds of insight around how to bring the essence of Buddhist meditation to mainstream society – released from its cultural and historic trappings and made accessible to the general public.

Kabat-Zinn, keen to apply his insight in practical ways, was able to persuade the authorities at the University of Massachusetts Medical School to let him use a room in the basement to receive referrals from doctors. He took on patients who were experiencing long-term pain and illness that had not been 'cured' by traditional medicine. People who were prepared to try something different. That 'something different' was a weekly session, with lots of home practice and exercises, drawn from yoga and meditation – particularly mindfulness meditation.

The 8-week course that Kabat-Zinn devised went on to become the Mindfulness Based Stress Reduction (MBSR) programme which today is taught by thousands of trainers in more than 30 countries worldwide. The University of Massachusetts Medical School Centre for Mindfulness alone has taken over 22,000 people through the 8-week course. Once a solid research base had been established, the MBSR framework and approach became the model for subsequent applications of mindfulness, which are used today in many different areas of mainstream mental health and medicine.

SO WHAT IS 'MINDFULNESS'?

> 'Mindfulness is the awareness that arises when we pay attention, on purpose, in the present moment, with curiosity and kindness to things as they are.'

This working definition framed by Kabat-Zinn does a good job of encapsulating the essential qualities of mindfulness. Mindfulness is not something we are 'taught' or 'given' as such; it's a natural capacity that we all have that may arise when we are deeply absorbed in something, or in a situation that demands our full attention. When people meditate they are cultivating the conditions that give rise to this mindful awareness.

All world religions contain elements devoted to reflection and to developing inner peace, but the Buddhist traditions seem to have especially focused on exploring these aspects of the human psyche. Mindfulness programmes draw on these explorations, but the competencies that are developed are naturally occurring, inherent, human capacities, and the courses for schools outlined in this book are completely secular.

Mindfulness is really the opposite of forgetfulness. We forget about what is happening right now because we are often busy thinking too much – worrying about the future or revisiting the past. 'Re-living and pre-living,' as Chris Cullen from the Oxford Mindfulness Centre puts it. When we train in mindfulness, we train in encountering the present moment, in making ourselves more available to what is happening *right now*. And, of course, the present moment is the only place where anything ever happens – so it's worth trying to spend more time here!

How Do We Do That?

You could be forgiven for believing that mindfulness and meditation are all about the mind, but in many ways, training in mindful awareness is often focused on the body - on consciously cultivating the connections between mind and body that can help us find greater balance in our everyday experiences and behaviours. While our *mind* might be off in the future, worrying or imagining, or back in the past, regretting or re-enacting, our *body* is only here in the present. So, on a basic level, if we train ourselves to be more directly connected with our bodies, then we can spend more time fully inhabiting our experience of life.

Modes of Mind

Let's take a moment to explore two key modes of brain functioning that are central to mindful awareness. Read the following passage, and as you read, take the time to allow yourself to imagine and 'feel' your way into the situation described. (This, by the way, is not a mindfulness exercise, it is a simple visualisation adapted from an example by David Rock, 2009.)

 THE JETTY

Imagine it's summertime and you are on a small jetty on the edge of a peaceful lake. You are sitting on the wooden boards, your legs dangling over the water. It's a warm day and you can feel the heat on your skin and face. There's a refreshing drink in your hand and you can feel the coolness of the glass contrasting with the heat of the day. A light breeze blows across the water, stirring your hair, and the hairs on your arms. The breeze carries a faint smell of reeds, earth and lake water.

A cloud passes over the sun and then a cooler breeze blows across the water and gives you a slight shiver, reminding you that the summer is passing quickly. The new school year will soon begin. You recall that you still have some course planning to do when you get back home. You start to wonder about the new classes you have to teach - 'Will the new text books arrive in time?' - and some of the jobs you left undone at the end of the year - 'I never did clean out those old files'.

Whether or not you actually 'felt' any sensations, you probably noticed what happened there. We moved from full-on present moment sensory experiencing into thinking - planning the future with our internal narrative mode. Figure 2.1 illustrates two primary modes of mind.

These two main modes of mind - **sensing** and **thinking** - can be observed in action using brain scans. We all have this capacity to experience our senses and to move into our thoughts and we flip from one to the other and back again, usually without even noticing. Most of us, however, spend a lot of time in our thoughts and

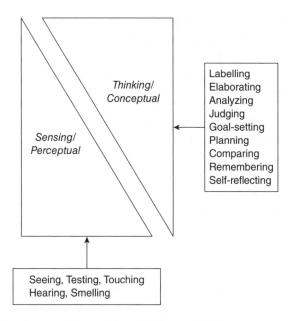

Figure 2.1   Modes of mind (adapted from Williams, 2010)

inner storytelling and not so much time experiencing the present moment directly through our senses.

A key component of training in mindful awareness is learning how to bring our attention out of thinking mode and into our bodies and senses – into sensing mode. We train for this not to stop our thinking, nor to be permanently in our bodies, but in order to have greater choice over where our attention goes. To be able to inhabit the full range of sensory *and* cognitive experiences, depending on what is most appropriate for the occasion. When we notice we are stuck in (or overwhelmed by) thinking, we can learn to drop our attention down into the body. When we want to focus on the future, to do some planning for example, then we can choose to do that with full consciousness, now, in this moment.

When we are having a difficult day – perhaps feeling stressed by an interaction with a parent or colleague, or under pressure from a pile of papers that need to be marked – we may be vaguely aware of discomfort, and that we are not really in the best state of mind to walk into a classroom. If, though, we have already established some mindfulness strategies, these may allow us to just take a moment to drop into sensing our body and breath, to acknowledge our thoughts and emotions, maybe take a deeper breath and let some of that tension go. We can thus make a small shift in our focus, even in a brief moment, that enables us to be more present with those students in front of us right now.

BEING WITH PAIN

By engaging in this type of focused, present moment awareness, many participants of those early courses created by Jon Kabat-Zinn found a significant difference in their experience of their illness or their pain. Some seemed to change their relationship with pain – to see themselves less defined by their illness and to find more optimism through regaining a more active role in their lives. Others seemed to actually experience less pain. This is not just a theory or an idea – the powerful combination of ancient practices with modern science reveals that, when trained in this way, changes can often be observed in the brain. Researchers are discovering that, even with initial adult mindfulness training, some significant alterations in the structure and wiring of the brain can be detected (Massachussetts General Hospital, 2011). The original purpose of meditation practices, at least in Buddhism, was to understand the causes of human suffering and how to end it. Modern applications of these ancient approaches appear to confirm the validity of these techniques in a scientific setting.

Pain and Suffering

So we know from the research and from people's experiences that something significant is happening here. But what are we actually doing that makes a difference? Common to many of these applications of mindfulness is a more active role on the part of the person who is suffering – a decrease in the passivity that often accompanies a medical diagnosis. There is also an aspect of being able to accept and work with our condition as it is, and the paradox is that sometimes this active acceptance can reduce the intensity of the experience.

BILLY AND THE MOSQUITO

Whilst I was in the process of re-discovering mindfulness in my middle age, I took my son, Billy, on a trip to Egypt. He was about 14 at the time and as excited as I was by the amazing sites, stories and people we encountered. One morning we rode camels up to the tombs in Luxor and then went on to do a tour of other nearby sites. As interested as he was in the ruins we were exploring, he was also plagued by some nasty mosquito bites that he just couldn't resist scratching. Eventually this started to interfere with the whole experience for him. In the midst of all the magnificent ancient splendour, the irritation caused by those tiny insects had, for him, taken centre stage. In the bus between two sites he was becoming increasingly annoyed, and having no cream with me I decided to try out one of the techniques I had been learning. (I guessed that his suffering might be sufficient to motivate him to try it!)

'Instead of letting this drive you crazy, do you want to try a different way of dealing with it?'

'Like what?'

'Don't scratch the bites for a bit and just sit upright, close your eyes and let yourself feel the itching ... Just breathe gently and deeply and close your eyes and focus on exactly the spot where you feel most irritation ... Now just keep breathing and noticing and let yourself fully sense what those bites feel like on your skin...

After a moment I asked him how it felt now.

'The itching has gone!'

After a while the itch returned, but it wasn't so intense and Billy was able to go onto the next site and enjoy the experience. He told me years later that he had imagined his breath going to the itching spot like those TV adverts for pain relief pills that target a throbbing red spot in the body. Whenever the itching returned that day, he would breathe into it and it would 'disappear' again for a while. He had learnt a new way of actively dealing with discomfort.

Of course I am not trying to compare the pain experienced from serious illnesses to the itch of a mosquito bite, and we can't all overcome pain simply by accepting it. But it is true that we often solidify, feed and even magnify our difficulties by the way we react to them. Exceptional people like Nelson Mandela and Viktor Frankl have shown how, even in the most awful of situations, some individuals have been able to choose an attitude that reduces and even transforms their suffering.

Perhaps a partial explanation of what might be happening here is encapsulated in the formula:

Suffering = Pain × Resistance

Or, as some put it, 'Pain in life is inevitable, suffering is optional'. We can't remove all negative experience from our lives, but we can at least 'work the edge' of how we are impacted by suffering – and especially how our story about pain and illness can sometimes add to, or feed, the experience of suffering.

TREATING PAIN

Over the last 30 years, research on the impact of MBSR courses on the experience of pain has increasingly shed light on the physiological and psychological processes involved. Here's one recent example:

The standard pharmaceutical approach to testing new drugs is to compare medications with a placebo, which we now know can have a significant effect itself and there have been some interesting research studies exploring placebo processes (Feinberg, 2013). In 2014 Fadel Zeidan and his team at Wake Forest Baptist Medical Centre in North Carolina, USA, designed an experiment to compare mindfulness meditation with a pain relief placebo (Zeidan et al., 2015). Participants were randomly trained either in mindfulness meditation or in how to use a neutral cream (the placebo) they could apply in case of burns. Later they were actually given a burn on their

(Continued)

(Continued)

arm in the lab and they then applied either the cream or their technique. The placebo cream significantly reduced pain sensation (-11 per cent) and unpleasantness (-13 per cent), but mindfulness meditation outscored the placebo effect in both categories (-27 per cent and -44 per cent).

Another group that was trained in a simple relaxation technique had a lower effect than the cream, but what surprised researchers the most was the way in which scans revealed that pain was being mediated in the brain:

'We were completely surprised by the findings. While we thought that there would be some overlap in brain regions between meditation and placebo, the findings from this study provide novel and objective evidence that mindfulness meditation reduces pain in a unique fashion.'

(Wake Forest Baptist Medical Center, 2015)

The conclusion from this study was that, 'Based on our findings, we believe that as little as four 20-minute daily sessions of mindfulness meditation could enhance pain treatment in a clinical setting'.

The application of mindfulness techniques in MBSR to treating pain, and the research that validated this, led to a flurry of studies, as illustrated in Figure 2.2. Mindfulness-based approaches have been researched with people with cancer,

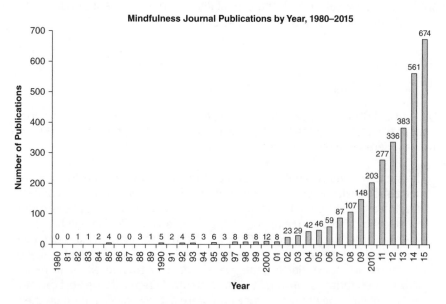

Figure 2.2 Exponential increase of mindfulness research publications since 2007/8 (American Mindfulness Research Association, 2016)

eating disorders, addictions and many other afflictions, often with significant results. In mental health, mindfulness has been used especially in treatment for depression, anxiety and stress. Mindfulness-Based Cognitive Therapy (MBCT), based on the MBSR programme, targets people suffering from clinical depression and has been particularly successful in this area.

FEELING YOUR FEET

OK, enough theory for now; let's try something more directly experiential. The only way to really understand mindfulness is to *experience* it. Because we are exploring non-verbal experience these words can only be guides – we are trying to see if we can put words aside for a while – or at least to turn *down* the volume on our thoughts a little, while turning *up* the volume on the senses. Let's see if we can let go of these ideas and thoughts for a moment and just play with inhabiting our sensory experience.

The best way to do this is with someone guiding you, so you might want to do this using the audio track in the 'Try It Out!' section at end of the chapter.

If you prefer to read the guide yourself, just use the cues below to steer yourself towards slowing down a little.

You will need a few minutes (approx. 3-5) and a quiet space to try this out. If you are not in a good situation to do this right now, no problem – you can choose a better time later.

 FEEL YOUR FEET ACTIVITY

If you are ready, start to build an intention to focus on this activity and to cue yourself as you read by:

Slowing down your reading a little,

... pausing every now and then ...

... seeing if you can notice

your body ...

....

Now,

... just gently trying to focus your attention

on sensing

(Continued)

(Continued)

your feet.

See if you can notice the feel of your socks or shoes,

perhaps how they hold or constrain your feet ...

Try to notice the temperature of your feet (warm or cool)

– and their weight (or lightness).

... Now noticing the connection with the surface beneath your feet.

....

Just pause your reading for a longer moment now, sensing again how your feet feel,

from the inside (close your eyes for a moment if it helps).

....

Try including with the feet a sense of the body sitting here supported by the chair beneath you.

(Close your eyes again if it helps.)

And now, while you slowly, softly read this,

see if you can also notice the breath moving in your body.

The physical sensations of breathing,

wherever you feel them most vividly ...

Just staying with the breath if you can for a few cycles ...

....

Finally, after reading this last part,

just for a minute, try

putting the book down,

feeling your breath, and your body,

letting your eyes move slowly around the room,

and gently allowing yourself to fully sense yourself,

sitting here in this room.

So how was that?

What did you notice?

Did you feel tired?

Or relaxed?

Could you stay with the sensations?

Did your mind keep wandering off?

Was it difficult to engage?

Maybe you couldn't feel your feet at all?

Or perhaps you were thinking 'What a waste of time!'

Any of these possibilities, along with a variety of others, could have been your experience during those few minutes. There is no right or wrong in these practices. At this stage we are learning to notice whatever we notice, so there's no need to feel that you got it 'wrong' if it was a struggle. We are just exploring, noticing what happens when we do try to move our attention into the body. If this is a new type of experience for you, as with any training of a new skill, it's important not to push too hard, not to be too self-critical. We can learn as much from challenging moments as we can from when things go more easily. We are just starting to work on building up our intention to pay attention.

WANDERING AND WONDERING

We worry about the future, obsess about the past, get drawn in by the mind's narrator, sometimes getting stuck on autopilot, not really paying attention to where we are and what we are doing. Even when focused on the present moment we may still have these, mostly subliminal, intermittent commentaries from our inner critic – we might be putting ourselves down ('I'm just not good/smart/strong enough') or puffing ourselves up, making comparisons with others and working out where we fit ('At least I'm not as ugly/short/tall/thin/fat/arrogant/shy/etc as him/her!').

Mindful awareness training can help us work with our wandering mind (and we all have one of those!), but this doesn't mean we can't appreciate and celebrate the wonders of mind wandering. Some of my best ideas have come when I let my mind wander and just see what turns up. Wisps of poetry, music or ideas might bubble up, sometimes as if from nowhere. It's true that, for me, most of the time when this happens I'm doing something physical at the time – walking, cycling, taking a shower, or maybe staring out of a train window and being gently rocked whilst travelling through the countryside. So I guess there's a degree of 'embodiment' even if I'm not focused on it. But this is different from the more 'disembodied', circuitous, thinking that can take over in the small hours of the morning or after a stressful day.

THE WORRY GENE

We are the descendants of Worriers as well as Warriors – it's those anxious genes that sometimes kept our ancestors alive and that have been passed down to us. I sometimes tell my students that my mother was a wonderful woman and also a great worrier and if there had been an Olympic competition for worrying my mum would have been able to represent Great Britain. 'And,' I tell them, 'I have inherited that capacity and perfected it – taken it to a whole new level.' Worrying comes easily to me – it's just the way my mind tends to go.

Because I am quite good at worrying it has been hardwired into my neurological circuitry. My habitual thought patterns travel down familiar inter-synaptic routes that have become well myelinated (insulated) through regular use. This makes it easier for the electro-chemical currents in my neurons to flow along these 'worryways'. Through training, however, I have learnt to notice this process and often now I can choose to *not* go down those default neural motorways and instead turn off down a gentler side road, one that is more conducive to having a calmer, more pleasant journey.

Most of us seem to have a built-in tendency to veer towards the negative when our thoughts are left to wander too long, and there's a danger of getting trapped in subliminal, negative thinking – especially when this is fuelled by an underlying low mood or a strong emotion such as fear, anger or sadness (Killingsworth and Gilbert, 2010). As cognitive behavioural therapists have discovered, sometimes our attempts to think our way out of a depression can just keep us stuck in a downward spiral. Training in mindfulness has helped me to notice the difference between pleasant or creative daydreaming and circuitous worrying which serves no positive purpose.

The wandering mind can be a creative or restorative state when we daydream (Callard and Margulies, 2011), or it can fuel negative states when we obsess or catastrophise. With time and patience we can train ourselves so that we can choose to allow it to wander or, if we notice it is causing us problems or undermining us, we can learn to gently pull ourselves out of thinking into the present moment, through the sensory anchors we have established in our practice.

> Meditators are not 'people whose minds don't wander';
>
> people meditate *because* minds wander.

When we see an image of a room full of meditators everyone appears to be so calm and serene, but the reality is that at any one moment each person could be experiencing anything across the full range of human emotions and sensations – not all of them calm or pleasant. It's important to understand how difficult it can sometimes be to just sit still quietly for a few minutes – especially if you might end up training students in this one day!

When we introduce adults and children to these practices, we take care to normalise their various experiences. The last thing we want is for young people to conclude, 'I tried mindfulness but it's not my thing, my mind wanders too much'. We help them understand the nature of the wandering mind – that it's just 'what minds do.'

In the next chapter we will explore in more depth establishing a personal mindfulness practice so that you can try this out for yourself. The more you practice, the more you are able to notice when the mind is fuelling worry, and then you can use your growing ability to focus your attention in ways that can help calm and centre yourself. Let's try a brief exploratory exercise, similar to the one we did earlier, but in a context you might be familiar with, just to give you an idea of how we might use mindful awareness for ourselves in school.

 ## BREATH BREAK

Imagine you've just come back to school after a week's holiday. You don't actually feel all that rested despite the break, and with reports to proofread and parent conferences coming up later this week, you feel unsure if you have sufficient energy to get you through this week. You certainly don't feel ready to face your class this morning – especially remembering the last lesson before the break, they were all over the place!

Then you remember that mindfulness exercise you have been practising and decide to give it a go now, even though it feels strange to do it in school. You turn your chair to face the window, look out over the trees at the clouds skimming across the apartments opposite.

Noticing the space above the crowded horizon, you take a deep breath.

You allow yourself to notice the cocktail of thoughts, feelings and sensations flowing around your mind and body. [Try this exercise now as you read – approx. 3 minutes]

Try to focus on *where* in the body you might notice any emotions or sensations. Then …

...Take a good long in-breath.

Allow yourself to notice the exhale,

encouraging a sense of letting go as you follow it out,

trying to feel the breath moving in your body,

closing your eyes for a moment if that helps.

Then gather your attention and take it down to your feet.

Feeling the feet inside your shoes.

And the floor under your feet.

Take a few breaths whilst focusing on the feet.

Now expand your attention to notice your legs, thighs and the feel of your body sitting here in the chair.

Being aware of your breath, raise your eyes and look out and around you for a moment.

Take one more deep inhale and exhale.

Maintaining some awareness of your body as best you can, get up slowly and prepare yourself to meet – and greet! – your students.

MINDFULNESS AND STRESS

The MBSR approach has been found to be highly effective for helping people deal with stress as well as pain. And it can be used as a preventative as well as a coping strategy. One piece of research (shown below) on using mindfulness for stress that might be of interest to those sceptical of 'self-report' studies was carried out with the US Marines and relied solely on physiological measures. (NB: In the following chapters we will look in more depth at using mindfulness to manage stress at work and beyond.)

MINDFUL MARINES

This study (Johnson et al., 2014) was done by researchers from the University of California, San Diego School of Medicine and the Naval Health Research Center:

- Four randomly selected platoons were assigned mindfulness training and four were assigned training-as-usual.

- The platoons were assessed before and after an 8-week mindfulness training course and also during and after a stressful combat training session some months later.

- Based on physiological blood, brain and heart markers, the results showed that 'mechanisms related to stress recovery can be modified in healthy individuals prior to stress exposure, with important implications for evidence-based mental health research and treatment.'

MINDFULNESS AND DEPRESSION

According to the World Health Organization, depression is one of the leading causes of global ill health (WHO, 2012). In recent years, psychologists have been developing some effective approaches to the treatment of depression that incorporate mindfulness. One major study recruited groups of people who had experienced clinical, recurring depression, and trained them on an 8-week mindfulness-based cognitive therapy (MBCT) course and then compared them with control groups (Teasdale et al., 2000). In this and similar, replicated studies, researchers have found that people with the MBCT training are half as likely to relapse into depression compared to control groups continuing their normal treatment. Whilst it may not work for everyone, MBCT does seem to offer a viable alternative to pharmacological options for reducing the reoccurrence of clinical depression, whilst avoiding any potential side-effects of medication. In fact, MBCT has become so well established now in the UK that the National Institute for Health and Clinical Excellence (2009) recommends it be prescribed by doctors as a National Health funded form of treatment for depression.

CHANGING THE BRAIN

- A 2007 study (Farb et al.), entitled 'Attending to the present: mindfulness meditation reveals distinct neural modes of self-reference', showed that mindfulness training increases 'viscero-somatic' processing and uncouples 'narrative-based' processing. In other words, the two modes of mind we explored earlier in the Jetty Scenario (**sensory mode** and **thinking mode**) can be more easily 'uncoupled' when we have trained ourselves to become more aware of physical sensations. It may be that for people who are depressed and prone to ruminate, this uncoupling helps them be aware of when an episode of depression might be beginning and then take steps to actively prevent relapse.

- A Massachusetts General Hospital study (2011) showed that after an 8 week mindfulness training programme (average 27 minutes practice per day), brain scans detected changes in the structure of the brain in those areas connected with emotional regulation and stress. The scans showed:

  o increased grey-matter density in the hippocampus (which can increase memory and learning capacities)

  o decreased grey-matter density in the amygdala (which can decrease our fear responses).

Understanding how rumination contributes to depressive states has implications for all of us – not just because depression is becoming such a common 21st-century affliction, but also because we all have to deal with negative moods and mind states. When we understand more about how our mind, body and emotions function, we are better positioned to learn strategies to deal with such difficulties.

HEALTHY SCEPTICISM

When we introduce mindfulness to teachers and students we encourage them to be 'healthily sceptical' about the research and about their expectations. Not to be so cynical or closed that you aren't prepared to try something a bit different, but not to be so open that you quickly conclude that mindfulness is the answer to all problems (actually, not many school-kids reach this conclusion, but it can happen with adults in mid-life).

Meditation may not always be the best option for everyone, depending on mental and physical circumstances. For example, someone with asthma may not feel comfortable with a focus on the breath, and it's important not to feel pressured to do so. (Although if you do have asthma and are interested, there has been some research done on how mindfulness may improve lung function and quality of life, [Pbert et al., 2012]). The MBCT programme has been proven to be effective for some people suffering from depression, but it is designed to be used as a preventative when in relapse, not when experiencing a major depressive episode.

WEBLINK: To see an example of someone trying a mindfulness experience with a 'healthily sceptical' outlook, check out this short film about CNN's Anderson Cooper:

http://www.cbsnews.com/news/the-newly-mindful-anderson-cooper/

Choosing what works for you is good practice in self-care. When we employ healthy scepticism we are prepared to try something and, even if at first it is a challenge, then we might choose to persist based on encouragement and guidance from others that we trust, or on our understandings from research. But ultimately, we are going to decide for ourselves, based on our own experience what works and what doesn't.

GOING PUBLIC

As results from scientific research spread, mindfulness became increasingly of interest to the general public. An MBCT book on *The Mindful Way Through Depression* (Williams et al., 2007) was followed in 2011 by a less clinical, more generally accessible book *Mindfulness: A Practical Guide to Finding Peace in a Frantic World* by Mark Williams and Danny Penman. This excellent self-directed 8-week course book has now been translated into more than 20 languages and is an international bestseller, showing that interest in mindfulness is coming not just from people who are clinically depressed or in pain. We are all in need of more space and downtime and many of us can benefit from practical guidance in how to achieve better balance in our lives. So, the combination of brain scan technology with the adoption and adaptation of Eastern traditional meditative practices in various secular forms in the West has opened up new horizons in mental and physical health. Exploring the benefits of these deep understandings of the human psyche without the trappings of organised religion has enabled a host of scientific research and new understandings in mental health interventions. Psychologists and educators have only recently begun to consider if the advances outlined above in applying mindful awareness training to mental and physical health could be of benefit to children and young people in schools.

MENTAL HEALTH AND YOUNG PEOPLE

A primary concern for us as teachers is the alarming rate of increase in mental health issues for children and young people:

- A meta-study in the USA found that children and college students in the 1980s were reporting average levels of anxiety higher than those of young psychiatric patients in the 1950s (Twenge, 2000).

- The onset of major depression is now most commonly reported to start in adolescence (Williams et al., 2012).

- According to a 2012 Chief Medical Officer report, 10 per cent of UK children have a diagnosable mental disorder (Murphy and Fonagy, 2012).

- In 2014 a survey of 830 USA college student counselling centres reported a 94 per cent growth of 'severe psychological problems'. These were mainly anxiety disorders and serious psychological crises that, according to one centre Director, have created a situation where counsellors 'can no longer do therapy ...[they] can only triage acute crises' (Gallagher, 2015).

- Self-harm rates among children and young people in the UK have increased sharply over the past decade (Murphy and Fonagy, 2012).

- The World Health Organization (2016) stated that 'depression is the top cause of illness and disability among adolescents and suicide is the third cause of death.' Suicide figures only indicate the tip of an iceberg of suffering amongst young people: in the USA among young adults (15-24 years) there is one suicide for every 100-200 attempts (Goldsmith et al., 2002).

We don't necessarily need surveys and statistics to convince us that lifestyles are out of balance these days – many of us have already either experienced mental illness ourselves or we know family, friends or students who have suffered or who are suffering. The World Health Organization (2016) advocates for education in this area to be augmented: 'Building life skills in children and adolescents and providing them with psychosocial support in schools and other community settings can help promote good mental health.'

Most of the research on mindfulness-based interventions has been done with adults but this situation is changing and research with young people and children, while still seen as an 'emergent field', is beginning to yield some positive indications. In Chapter 5 we will look at some of this research evidence and explore how some teachers have begun to adapt adult mindfulness programmes for children and teenagers in schools.

In this chapter we have focused on the use of mindful awareness training in medicine and mental health but I want to conclude by emphasising that it's not all about dealing with difficulty and avoiding despair or the problems of life – this work is just as much about enjoying life and appreciating the wonderful opportunity to be alive on this beautiful planet. Mindful awareness training can help us with challenging experiences and with difficult emotions, thoughts and sensations, but we can also use it simply for the ease and joy of slowing down, being more in our bodies and being more able to appreciate the present moment.

'Oh, I've had my moments, and if I had to do it over again, I'd have more of them. In fact, I'd try to have nothing else. Just moments, one after another, instead of living so many years ahead of each day.'

Nadine Stair, 85 years old (quoted in Kabat-Zinn, 1991)

WHAT REALLY MATTERS?

- The ancient art of cultivating mindful awareness is being applied in mainstream medicine and mental health with proven impact on pain, anxiety and depression.

- This is now leading to a range of initiatives in educational settings exploring the potential for positive mental health applications for young people and teachers.

TRY IT OUT!

- If you didn't yet try the activity on page 21, then consider setting aside 10 minutes sometime this week to slowly go through the exercise; alternatively, follow a guided audio version at www.mindwell-education.com.

- In the following chapters we look at specific ways to develop various mindful awareness practices. For now, if you want to explore a little, consider building a quiet moment into your day. Here are a few suggestions to choose from to get you started:

  o Take two minutes, maybe after you shower and before your breakfast, to just sit quietly and take a few conscious breaths. You don't have to sit cross-legged on the floor, a normal chair will also do.

  o If you normally drink tea or coffee in the morning, consider using this time to simply sit and sense, enjoying the experience of drinking rather than planning your day or reading the paper while you drink.

  o Set a timer for 5 minutes and sit quietly, sensing the body and feeling the movement of breathing wherever you can notice it. Expect the mind to wander off and when you notice it has, gently bring your attention back to the physical sensations of breath or body.

  o Try using the audio link as a daily guided settling (approx. 5 minutes).

With all these exercises remember to be kind to yourself – don't beat yourself up if it doesn't work out as you hoped or planned! Remember the qualities of mindfulness we are seeking to cultivate:

'Mindfulness is the awareness that arises when we pay attention, on purpose, in the present moment, with **curiosity** and **kindness** to things as they are.'

FURTHER READING AND RESOURCES

Kabat-Zinn, J. (1991) *Full Catastrophe Living: How to Cope with Stress, Pain and Illness using Mindfulness Meditation*. London: Piatkus.

A fascinating insight into Jon Kabat-Zinn's MBSR approach and a great introduction to mindfulness. You can see a touching film of his early work in:

Healing and the Mind with Bill Moyers (1993) Public Broadcasting Service
https://vimeo.com/39767361

Williams, M., Teasdale, J., Segal, Z. and Kabat-Zinn, J. (2007) *The Mindful Way Through Depression: Freeing Yourself from Chronic Unhappiness*. New York: Guilford Press.

Contains an outline for a self-directed course and many insights into the use of MBCT to treat depression.

Gunaratana, B. (2011) *Mindfulness in Plain English*. Somerville, MA: Wisdom.

An accessible and illuminating guide to meditation from a well-regarded Buddhist author.

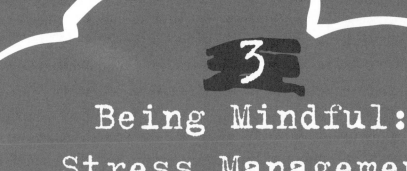

3

Being Mindful: Stress Management and Self-care

This chapter:

↘ looks at the conscious practice of developing and applying mindful awareness to daily life

↘ considers how such training can help us manage stress and why a focus on self-care is such a key element for teachers

↘ introduces practical examples and ideas for both formal and informal mindfulness practice.

TEACHER SELF-CARE

As teachers, we are members of 'the caring professions' - a group that includes doctors, nurses and social workers. For many this career path is a vocation, a calling - a gift even. We may feel privileged to be entrusted with the care, growth and learning of our students, and we may find meaning and purpose in our daily efforts to nurture the next generation. As educators we give a lot: we invest our time and energy in our work, and we give something personal of ourselves to our students. This may often feel stimulating and rewarding, but over time we may also be in danger of burnout. There is always more to be done, more meetings to attend, more emails to respond to, more duties to take on, better ways of teaching things. At the end of the day we may feel fulfilled and inspired, but we may also feel drained and exhausted. Teaching can be both nourishing and depleting, and if the overall balance swings towards the latter, sustainability and health can be at risk. Knowing how best to deal with these demands and to manage stress not only helps us avoid burnout, it can also enhance our teaching skills.

> **'Keeping your own wellbeing in mind is essential to create the experiential conditions to inspire students to learn.'**

This quote is from Daniel Siegel's preface to *The Social Neuroscience of Education* by Louis Cozolino (2013). Siegel is not just expressing an opinion as a professor of psychiatry; he is also summarising the findings of Cozolino's book.

Thanks to scientific exploration of the importance of relationship in learning, we now understand much more about early development through the process of attachment to our primary caregivers. Young humans are predisposed to connect with adults on many subtle levels. When a teacher is in a room with a group of children, they step into this evolutionary predisposition. This means that, in addition to the academic, analytical and conceptual content that the teacher is focusing on, their students are also cueing into a range of bodily, sensory and emotional cues.

Our engagement in the present moment and our authentic connection to ourselves and others has a significant, often unrecognised impact on the efficacy of our teaching, and of course on the learning of our students. Much of this is subliminal, but the research is pointing us to an understanding that:

> **How** we teach is as important as **what** we teach.

THE OXYGEN MASK

As a parent on a plane our instinct might be to help our children first if there was a problem, but we are instructed to get our own oxygen supply sorted before we help others. Many mindfulness teacher-training programmes use this metaphor because as teachers it is often easier for us to focus on the needs of our students than on our own needs. But it is only when we know how to take care of ourselves – to nourish ourselves and to find balance – that we can effectively model these skills and help develop them in our students.

In 2012 I helped establish MindWell (mindwell-education.com), a small organisation that supports schools and institutions seeking to establish mindfulness, social-emotional learning and wellbeing in their communities. We created the framework below to help us structure our work with educators:

Three Aspects of Mindfulness in Education

Be mindful

Teach mindfully

Teach mindfulness

- The basis for all of our work in this area is *being mindful*.
- The heightened awareness that arises from developing a mindfulness practice will often impact the way we are in the classroom, enabling us to *teach* more *mindfully*.
- Once we have this foundation, we may choose to train to *teach mindfulness* to others.

As our mindfulness practice grows, we can tune in to the body more and also become more sensitively attuned to the classroom environment, and to our interactions. Noticing our physical responses to stressors can make us more aware of tensions that could develop over time into ill-health, and so we can use this awareness to try to take better care of ourselves. When we focus more on self-care we become better connected with ourselves, which leads to better relationships with students. This in turn can improve their learning. Being more mindful in our daily lives can help us sustain ourselves and maintain our health, vitality and engagement in this wonderful and demanding profession.

If new teachers can learn some of these skills whilst in initial teacher training and also then work in schools that are supportive of teacher self-care, it is likely that more teachers will be better equipped to thrive and remain longer in the profession. We will take up this theme further in Chapter 4.

Being mindful arises out of our own personal mindfulness practice – both **formal** (sitting meditation, body scans etc.) and **informal** (bringing mindful awareness into our daily activities and into our relationships). Our own mindfulness underlies all other aspects of mindfulness in education, but this does not mean we need to be a perfectly enlightened being before we can start training children. It just means that whatever we attempt to do with students we have already attempted for ourselves.

> There is not one way in which I believe mindfulness couldn't be profoundly valuable for children ... if it's done in the right way. And if it's not done in the right way it would be a travesty to actually do it, so we have to proceed very sensitively in that regard. (Kabat-Zinn, 2013)

Some teachers might feel frustrated because they get enthused about mindfulness, want to get trained up to teach it to students, but then discover there are significant prerequisites they have to meet to be accepted on some courses. Or they may eventually do a training course and want – or are expected – to train up other teachers right away, as we do with most forms of professional development – but this is not your average professional development course. If you want to eventually train students it is important to take your time, go slowly and wait to really establish your own personal practice first. Otherwise, despite best intentions, it is possible that you might even turn some children off the idea.

SUPPORTING TEACHER SELF–CARE IN SCHOOLS

The central theme of this book, that a *focus on teacher self-care needs to precede everything else*, is not a message we are used to hearing in schools. For school leaders who really appreciate the importance of valuing teachers, it becomes clear that schools need to look at how they can best facilitate this. It does not mean schools have to be directly responsible for the nourishment of their teachers, it's more that we need to be explicit and proactive in creating conditions in schools that encourage and promote teacher self-care. When leaders and parents understand the importance of this they can support initiatives that enable teachers to develop these capacities in themselves, and teachers can then model and teach them to their students.

'Developing groundedness and not allowing myself to be pulled around by the wind is all down to the learning I've done through mindfulness and the daily practice helps with that. We do work hard and it's a career that sucks a lot out of you. You have to give a lot of yourself and those moments of stillness feel like recharging. The job requires you to be so sociable and I'm actually quite introverted. I recharge through being on my own – and doing that mindfulness practice sometimes feels like the equivalent of half a day's walk out in the hills.'

Primary School Teacher, UK

Some schools are already providing professional development funds for teachers to take an MBSR, MBCT or similar course for themselves. A few even pay for, or contribute to, subscriptions for teachers to access apps such as Headspace or other programmes that can help them develop a daily meditation practice. Some teachers do go on to train students, but that is not the only reason to support such programmes. Enlightened leaders can recognise the value of teachers knowing how to manage their stress, relate more sensitively to colleagues, parents and students, and hone their classroom and behavioural management skills through enhanced self-awareness and classroom presence.

'Mindfulness helped me personally balance that busy workload with the needs of the pupils. School can be a hectic place but I'm reminded of a quote I heard that really helped me to focus on the pupils – "I used to get annoyed by interruptions until I realized that interruptions were my day". The mindfulness approach helped me to be very present with people rather than get on with the 15 reports I had to write. You can learn to notice in yourself if you are getting anxious and actually become aware of when you get the first pangs of it being stressful. I never thought about it in that way before. Noticing any ruminations and having a period of settling kept my inner compass in the right direction.'

Liz Lord, Special Educational Needs Coordinator, UK

STRESS

For teachers, the need to be 'on' all day whilst teaching, the number of decisions to be made in a day, the lesson preparation and extracurricular duties, recording and reporting, dealing with students, parents and colleagues and so on, all make it necessary for us to know how to be able to sustain and take care of ourselves.

One of the key problems for 21st-century humans is that our physiology responds to mental and emotional stressors as much as it does to physical threat. Our response systems can be activated when we open up our inbox and see the long list of unread messages, or even by just *thinking about* our overwhelmingly long 'to-do' list. For many of us these days psychological and social stressors are much more common than physical ones. Just see if you can notice what happens when you slowly read the words and phrases below. Allow each to sink in a little and see if you can pick up any subtle sensations in your body:

emails,

deadlines,

family responsibilities,

to-do lists,

lack of time

A 'NEW NORMAL'

In the presentations that he does for schools, Tim Burns (founder of Educare) talks about a 'new normal' that society is adapting to in terms of stress levels (see Figure 3.1).

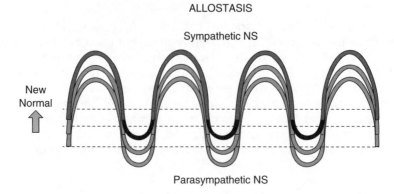

Figure 3.1 Chronic elevated stress levels – a new normal (courtesy of Tim Burns, *www.timburnseducare.com*)

The Physiology of Balance and Stress

The physiological state of our body is normally self-regulating and a key factor in maintaining this state of balance is the autonomic nervous system (ANS). The ANS comprises two contrasting systems that give us energy when we need it, or slow us down when we don't:

- the sympathetic nervous system (SNS) is our accelerator pedal
- the parasympathetic nervous system (PNS) is our intelligent braking system.

When we have to cope with an emergency such as a tiger stalking us in the bush, or suddenly having to meet a moved deadline, the blood is instantly filled with glucocorticoids and other hormones that rush around the body mobilising our response resources. When the SNS pushes us into action it uses up valuable fuel so the PNS needs to slow things down, calm us and give us the ability to digest and store energy and bring us back to balance. As we can see in Figure 3.1, the upper curves (symbolising activation for action by the SNS) are longer than the lower curves (rest and recovery through the PNS). Our lifestyles are engaging the SNS more than they do the PNS, creating a long-term imbalance that starts to feel almost 'normal' – or, just 'the way things are'.

So, these systems that evolved to cope with physical threat prime us to be ready for action the moment we detect an unusual rustle in the jungle, physical or mental. *But most of us are not hardwired to deal efficiently with the pace and frequency of modern psychological threats.* Long term, these over-activated stress responses put too much strain on the system. Even if we get a short holiday we don't always unwind enough to fully relax. Sometimes it's just easier to keep ourselves hyped-up rather than cope with the initial discomfort of slowing down and recognising how tired or stressed we are.

A degree of stress is helpful and necessary. **Eustress** is the technical term for positive stress (we usually call it 'stimulation'), and in Chapter 4 we look at how

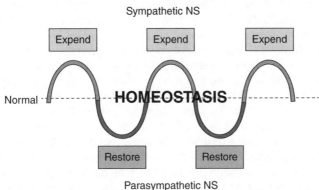

Figure 3.2 Homeostasis (courtesy of Tim Burns, www.timburnseducare.com)

developing awareness of our stress indicators can be very useful in our teaching. But our stress responses evolved for short-term use in physical situations and the harmful effects of long-term stress are well documented. Because these days few of us are getting enough 'rest and recovery' (R&R) time we need to take conscious, intentional action if we want to restore balance (see Figure 3.2).

DE–STRESSING

For sure there are many ways to de-stress. Perhaps you run, walk, swim, play golf, go to the gym, do yoga, garden, gossip, cry, laugh, dance, bathe, drink, share, eat, switch off, or even shout!

It is so important for us to find and nurture healthy ways of coping with stress. It is worth noting that many of the typical ways of relaxing and de-stressing involve physical activity – getting back into the body. Alcohol can relax us too and can certainly get us 'out of our heads', though not always in such a restorative manner!

This offering from a secondary teacher colleague illustrates the point:

For a majority of my teaching career, I would come home and have a few drinks to unwind in the evenings. Because my mind and body had been so busy during the day, I needed something to 'take the edge off,' and help me relax and wine seemed to be the way to do it. I would drink wine while watching TV or spending time on my computer. I never really thought much about it and continued in that

(Continued)

(Continued)

pattern for a few years. After a time, however, I started to notice some effects – foggier in the mornings, a low level of constant sadness and a vague sense of regret, which I attributed to feeling like I was 'wasting my evenings', as they would dissolve into bedtime with no real sense of having lived. What had originally been a strategy for rest and recovery became more of a coping mechanism than a relaxation technique. I was losing my engagement with myself and my life. I certainly didn't feel refreshed the next morning. At the same time I had been developing a meditation practice and this helped me to begin to notice this pattern, to be gentle with myself about it and to slowly shift to healthier strategies for managing my stress.

How did I actually achieve that balance, you might wonder? I think it was a combination of factors – having the intention to cut down on the amount of wine that I drank, establishing a meditation practice which helped me recognise my thoughts and desires more clearly, and a very practical suggestion from a friend. She suggested that I take a breath before pouring myself a drink. And the next time, to take two breaths. Simple, right? Well, many times I forgot, but once I established the routine of doing this, it helped me work consciously with my engrained habit. Just taking a breath helped me to pause and reflect before the action so I could make an informed decision about whether or not I really wanted that drink. Don't get me wrong – I still love my wine! – but I'm able to be more balanced about it.

RE-BALANCING

Mindful awareness exercises activate the PNS and also tend to naturally deepen our breathing as we learn to let go more and re-balance our physiology. The natural physiological flow of activity and rest, of activation and relaxation, can be seen even in the space of a single breath. When we breathe in we activate the SNS and minutely raise our heart rate. When we breathe out we engage the PNS and minutely lower our heart rate (Sapolsky, 2004).

I have found from my own meditation practice that after 15–20 minutes or so of sitting my body usually begins to feel warm and relaxed, but I had wrongly assumed that following the breath was only about maintaining attention on a sensory object in order to train the mind. I now realise that whilst building a capacity to attend through focusing on breathing we are also treating our physiology to some much needed R&R time!

LEARNING TO COPE – A TEACHER'S STORY

As a young teacher I spent a lot of time crying – on the way to school, at school, on the way home from school ... I was so stressed out and overwhelmed that in my third year teaching I went part-time just so I could get my bearings. I carried on but had to stop again a few years later when difficulties arose in my personal life. I went through a divorce and soon after my father passed away. I needed time to cope with all of this. My father had introduced me to meditation in my early 20s but I never pursued it fully. It was at this time that I revisited some of the skills and concepts he taught me.

After a while, I noticed an impact on my professional life. I remember thinking one day at school, 'Hey, I'm not crying anymore between classes!'. The practices that I was doing for my own mental health and peace of mind were having a positive impact on my teaching. Because I was more connected with myself, I was able to be more connected with my students. We were able to create trusting relationships which allowed for deeper learning to occur. Teaching was still challenging, but something had shifted. I was able to be more calm and present with my students and was also able to notice when I was getting frustrated or irritated with them and/or colleagues, but instead of reacting without thinking which could often get me into trouble, I was able to respond with a more balanced approach. What's more, I actually began to really enjoy time with my students!

Mindfulness also allowed me to notice when I was pushing myself too hard. With heightened awareness of how my mind, body and emotions work together, I was able to notice my stress accumulating and make the choice to care for myself, which in turn, really helped me to care for my students. Mindfulness is the practical tool that helped me be a better teacher, and a better friend to myself.

Canadian High School teacher, Amy Burke

You can hear more about how mindfulness helped Amy in her TEDx Talk at https://www.youtube.com/watch?v=2i2B44sLVCM&t=1s&ab_channel=TEDxTalks

MINDFUL STRESS MANAGEMENT

So let's take a look at stress management by reflecting first on these two questions:

- What stresses *you* out?
- Where do you notice stress responses in your body?

We can become more aware of our typical *stress signature* and use the body as an early warning radar system to prevent us from being driven by unacknowledged tensions. You can start to try tuning in and recognising your familiar responses to stress – especially noticing (with an open curiosity in the moment if you can muster it) *where* you experience stress responses in your body. The first and crucial step in self-care is this recognition – accepting when stress is present in the body, and becoming aware of where you are experiencing it. The next step is doing something about it.

Developing a mindful awareness practice can add a valuable tool to your stress-management toolkit – one you can consciously engage in even when physical outlets are not available. Mindfulness is a portable skill that can be employed at any time. It's also possible to combine mindful awareness with your preferred unwinding mechanism to enhance the experience – you can cycle more mindfully, run mindfully, eat mindfully and even drink wine more mindfully!

 BREATHING TECHNIQUE – THE 7/11 (1–3 MINUTES)

From the feedback we have received, this simple technique has been the most popular of all with students and teachers when it comes to needing a quick way to try to settle nerves before an exam, speech, performance or other stressful moment.

- On an inhale, count to 7 and on the next exhale count to 11. *Try to match the count to the breath rather than forcing the breath to fit the count* – it's fine to speed up the rate of counting if you need to get up to 11.

- Sometimes when really stressed even trying to breathe and count to 11 can feel like a stressor, so you can also just silently speak the syllables:

  Sev – en ... Ee – Lev – en ...

  This is effectively a count of 2 in and 3 out.

- Whichever you do, make sure you actually pay attention to the counting because this can help unplug from the 'story' about the event or feeling.

- Do about three or four of these, really focusing on the breath and the counting and note any differences after.

- Repeat as often as necessary!

The 7/11 is a subtle but effective way of extending our exhalation a little. When we are stressed we seem to hold energy inside and in the upper part of the body – imagine the sharp intake of breath after a shock. When we sigh, we do so on a long exhale, letting go and activating the parasympathetic nervous system that can lower the heart rate a little and help to calm us.

(NB: 7/11 breathing is commonly used in therapy and there are various ways of doing it. The version described here is based on the approach taken in the Mindfulness in Schools Project's '.b' Programme.)

RESEARCH ON TEACHER STRESS AND MINDFULNESS TRAINING

Looking to support the establishment of more Directors of Wellbeing in schools, Nuffield Health (UK) were surprised to find that a common answer to the question they put to students:

'What are the major impacts on your sense of wellbeing in school?'

was:

'How stressed my teacher is today.'

There is a huge body of research on stress and its impact in various contexts:

- Around 40 per cent of USA teachers leave during the first 5 years. (Ingersoll and Stuckey, 2014)

- 82 per cent of UK teachers are suffering from lack of sleep and over three quarters from anxiety. Almost half of teachers in the last year have sought medical advice, over a third have taken medication, 5% have been hospitalised. Over three quarters of women teachers report that the job has affected their mental health and well-being. (NASUWT, 2016)

One common cause of teacher burnout is the stress that can be brought on from repeatedly dealing with difficult students and difficult situations (Kyriacou, 2001). In Chapter 4 we look at a new approach in teacher training in Denmark that is using mindfulness in initial teacher training to help teachers cope better with challenging moments and behaviour management. Another piece of action research that connected teachers, stress and mindful awareness training was carried out in 2011 with very positive indications as the following research shows.

A significant piece of research incorporating compassion training with mindful awareness training (Kemeny et al., 2011) randomly assigned 82 teachers to a training group or control group and found that after 8 weeks, those in the contemplative/emotion training group had:

- less negative emotion

- reduced feelings of depression

- increase in positive states of mind.

Follow-up research with participants found that after 5 months those in the training group had:

- lower blood pressure

- recovered from stressful task more quickly

- greater feelings of compassion towards others

- less hostility or contempt.

(NB. The 'lessening of hostility or contempt' factor was measured in connection with spouses and partners, illustrating the value this can have for those we relate to at home as well as at work!)

Further research on teachers, stress and wellbeing can be found in a very informative paper by Professor Katherine Weare, 'Evidence for mindfulness: impacts on the wellbeing and performance of school staff' (2014).

Mindfulness was very helpful in my life. I learned it not for teaching but because I needed it - about 7 years ago when I was doing my Masters degree, I got insomnia. It was quite serious and my friend introduced me to mindfulness and I did the MBSR course. Since then my insomnia has reduced a lot and my stress levels have been alleviated. I find it has helped me in my work as well. Sometimes when I talk to parents or I give some advice or consultation I think that I can empathise with them more and also when I give consultations I can appreciate their effort or be more accepting of their difficulties. My empathy has been enhanced.

Stanley Chan, Educational Psychologist, Hong Kong

BEING MINDFUL

Managing our stress is crucial in sustaining our effectiveness as educators and it can be practically supported through developing a mindfulness practice. We can separate ways of being mindful into 'formal' and 'informal' practices.

Formal Practice

A formal meditation practice is the bedrock of developing mindfulness. Here you are taking the time to pause, to really allow yourself to take a breath, and to begin to awaken and amplify your intrinsic capacity to be more mindfully aware. We will look at three different approaches to formal practice.

1. Sitting Meditation

In sitting meditation, the main intention is to find a place and a posture that will promote a relaxed alertness so you can simply sit still and undisturbed for a little while. Be reasonable about the time you set aside for practice at the beginning. You don't train for a marathon by running 42 kilometres the first day. Starting with even 2-5 minutes can be helpful as you establish a new routine and healthy habit. And if every day seems too much to start with, try with every other day at the beginning.

Although it can be challenging to sit still and we may go through stages of lethargy, discomfort or difficult emotions, it's also important, especially at the beginning, to enter into this gently. We also need to appreciate and enjoy it wherever possible - although we aim to be open to all our experiences, we are not doing this in order to feel miserable!

Establishing a good posture makes all the difference. I have found that sitting has improved my core muscles and made it easier to get a straighter uplift in my spine, but you may find at the beginning (like me) that if your core muscles are not strong it will take a little time before you can feel good just sitting and breathing.

You don't have to sit cross-legged on the floor. At first I sat in a chair and used the chair back for support. Now I am comfortable sitting forward on the edge of a chair or on a kneeling stool or cushion. Patience and kindness are the keys here.

With students, I get them to try out three postures (in the first exercise below) and to notice what message each sends to the mind and body (and see which are most helpful in supporting an intention to stay awake). Perhaps play with this for a moment yourself.

PLAYING WITH POSTURE (2 MINUTES)

- First, if you are sitting in a chair allow yourself to slouch completely, adapting as slovenly a position as you can. Exaggerate the posture and stay there for a moment or two.

- What message does this body position send to the mind?

- In a short while you will probably begin to feel like dozing off.

- Now try sitting bolt upright, military style, straight-backed, everything alert. Hold that for a moment.

- How did that feel?

- Awake and uptight perhaps? Certainly here you are giving a more vigilant message to the mind, but how sustainable is this position?

- Finally, Goldilocks style, we can seek an in-between position that's 'just right'.

- Sitting well, with both feet flat on the floor, small of the back away from the edge of the back of the chair (if you can manage that), a sense of being rooted through the feet to the floor and supported in the chair by the 'sit bones' and buttocks.

PREPARING TO SIT (2 MINUTES)

- Along with this sense of being grounded, bring a gentle uplift through the spine, allow the belly to come forward a little, and a soft curve in the small of the back. Check the shoulders are down, back and relaxed, not hunched. Tuck in the chin slightly and allow the head to feel supported by the spine, with an upward lift from the top of the head towards the ceiling.

- Maintain alertness while relaxing into this position.

- Checking perhaps with a slight swaying and rocking that the spine is central and that the breath is free to come and go.

- When you're in position and ready to start the sit you can gently close your eyes if that feels comfortable or just lower the gaze to a metre or so in front on the floor, softening the eyes.

So, you're ready to sit, but what do you do? Here are some introductory suggestions for developing a formal sitting practice.

SITTING PRACTICE STARTERS

- *Get a timer*: I use one called Insight Timer on my phone. It's a useful free tool that includes many guided meditations.

- *Use guided meditations*: At least at first. Maybe even from the start try alternating guided sessions one day and the next unguided using the timer, perhaps with a few random bells set to help bring you back from time to time. (See 'Try It Out' at the end of this chapter for some guided meditation examples.)

- *Seek guidance*: Join a sitting group or meditation centre to experience communal sitting and to get some supervision.

- *Go on a retreat*: Once you have established the basics of a mindfulness practice, consider going on a meditation retreat. It is really the longer retreats that provide the best opportunities to truly stop, allow inner processes to unfold and sit in a safe, supported, space. Guidance from experienced meditators can be extremely valuable, especially if your experiences ever become overwhelming at times.

- *Just sit*: Even if you don't feel like it, even if you have not managed it for a few days, just sit! As with creating any new habit or learning any new skill, a formal sitting practice does require a certain amount of discipline.

- *Create a designated place for sitting*: Making the space comfortable and inviting can be very helpful in establishing a new routine.

- *Renew your intention daily*: Remember your reasons for why you are developing this skill.

- *Be kind to yourself* when you don't manage to meet your expectations. Building self-compassion is a key element of this work.

Intention and attention

As you develop your personal practice the interplay between intention and attention becomes increasingly important. Setting a clear intention before you sit helps remind you where you want your attention to come back to when the mind starts to wander or when doubts appear.

Noticing when you have lost, and when you regain, attention can help reinforce your growing capacity to sustain focus. It's common for many of us at first to highlight the times when we *lose* attention: 'There I go again .... My mind just goes off every few seconds. I can't do this properly.' But we can, over time, see that noticing when you have lost attention is, itself, a positive occurrence. For each time you lose attention, there are an equal number of times when you regain it.

Health Warning – there may be times when meditation is not the best thing for you. As meditation teacher Malcolm Huxter advises,

> If you are prone to, or suffer with a clinical condition such as severe depression, debilitating anxiety or some form of psychosis, guidance and tailoring the practices may be important for you. Even if you do not suffer with a clinical condition it is important that you approach the exercises wisely and with moderation, and guidance from someone who has experience is always helpful. (2016: 5)

As always, self-care is the priority, and sometimes taking care of yourself may include *not* meditating or making sure you are supported by a suitably trained and experienced teacher of meditation.

2. The Bodyscan

MBSR programmes help people learn to manage stress and pain, and the core formal practice used is the **bodyscan**. Participants follow a daily guided tour of the body that opens up mind–body connections and helps create a different way of responding to life's stresses and physical difficulties. The challenge for most of us at the beginning is being able to stay awake whilst lying on your back in a comfortable position, with a soothing voice guiding you to 'aim and sustain' your attention on various parts of the body. But persistence certainly seems to pay off for most people and over time it gets easier to stay with the focus for longer.

I mentioned earlier my natural tendency to worry about things. It's almost a default mode. In retraining and re-wiring long-term habits, formal meditation practices like the bodyscan can really help create alternative default pathways. I have found that my body seems to appreciate getting this attention in bodyscans, and now it sometimes rewards me with pleasant sensations – reduced tension, warmth and tingles that I hadn't noticed before. As we build our capacity to attend we may also become more able to stay with sensations and tensions when they are *not* pleasant – to turn towards them with an open, accepting awareness.

To get started on bodyscans consider using one of the suggestions in 'Try It Out' at the end of this chapter.

3. Mindful Walking

A third common formal practice is **mindful walking**, which is really a walking meditation. Some people find it infuriating at first to slow down their walking, or to be walking without a destination, whereas for some mindful walking becomes the most powerful of introductory techniques that helps bring our attention into the body and the present moment. I was once on an intensive MBSR training retreat at OMEGA Institute in New York state. There were over a hundred participants, many of them completely new to meditation. A Spanish woman who was sitting next to me returned from the first 10-minute mindful walking practice and described in broken English a transformative experience she had had, simply due to slowing down and getting a fresh perspective on walking – and on a deeper level with her own sense of time and self.

To get started on mindful walking consider using one of the guided suggestions in 'Try It Out' at the end of this chapter.

Informal Practice

Perhaps the most appealing aspects of mindfulness for many people are its adaptability and portability. When we find ways to bring a more mindful awareness into our everyday activities it can be highly refreshing, and even profoundly liberating. Zen Master Thich Nhat Hanh says meditation is like winding up a dynamo – its effect goes beyond the sit and into our lives. The primed dynamo of attention keeps bringing us back from thought realms into the present moment, into mindful awareness.

Bringing more mindful attention into our day is known as **informal practice**. Here too *intention* is the key.

> I was rediscovering mindfulness for myself whilst I was working as Middle School Principal and at the beginning I found it very challenging to bring my practice into my workday. I would sit formally once or twice a week in a session offered to teachers after school by one of my colleagues, Tony Ackerman. Often it would be just Tony and me after a hectic school day. I perfected the art of falling asleep while sitting upright. From time to time I would jerk suddenly awake as my body executed a startle reflex and I would find myself in the silence of Tony's music room or listening to his gentle voice leading me through an exercise I had almost completely missed. Over time my tendency to doze off lessened and I found it easier to stay awake through the sessions.
>
> As a busy administrator, I knew it would be good for me now and then to take a good conscious breath, a full inhale and full exhale, so I often set that intention for my working day. But even so it was totally possible for me to go through the entire day in an adrenaline-caffeine-fuelled, fast-paced way without ever actually taking that one breath.
>
> How crazy is that?

There is something quite addictive and compelling about certain kinds of stress – it can feel (probably through dopamine stimulation) quite rewarding. We often just don't want to stop or even slow down. But it's better to learn to do so voluntarily now, than to find yourself being forced to slow down through ill-health or burnout in the future. *So what can we do to punctuate our days with some mindful moments?*

Here are some suggestions you can try during the day to help you remember to come out of autopilot or overthinking and back to the present moment.

WEAVING IT IN

- Post-it Note reminders – e.g. on mirrors or your laptop screen.
- Interval or random bell/chime apps on computers.
- Choosing to take a breath before sending an email.
- While walking, putting awareness into the hands and arms or feet.
- Use certain places as reminders to feel the body and breath, such as
  - walking from the car to the front door of school
  - walking through a threshold and taking a breath
  - slowing down a little in hallways or on the stairs.
  - popping outside for a breath of fresh air.

It's often said that 'Mindfulness is simple but it isn't easy', and this is so true for all of us when it comes to establishing a regular practice and bringing it more into our day. You may have many good intentions and, if you're like me, frequently fail to realise them. Patience, persistence and clear intent are highly valuable allies in helping us to continue to evolve more mindful ways of living and working so that over time these new, positive habits become more routine and less of a challenge.

When I first started to try taking a two- or three-minute breathing space in my office during the day, I would sit upright at my chair with my hand on my computer mouse in case anyone came in. 'How crazy,' I thought, 'that no one seems to mind too much that we all participate in a culture that promotes an overly fast pace of life, but I'm embarrassed to be seen taking a momentary break that could help me be a better administrator. What is *that* about?'

Eventually I did find things got a lot easier. In sitting meditations I didn't feel tired. I could take conscious pauses most days and the body scans I had been doing seemed to really kick in and help rewire my circuitry. Sometimes I didn't even have to remember to do anything – I would walk the hallways between meetings and my arms or legs might start to tingle of their own accord, reminding me that I actually do have a body, and recalling me from the incessant mulling over of whatever was preoccupying me that day; pulling me out of thinking about the last meeting or planning the next, back into sensing mode for a moment. Such informal practices were highly beneficial to me (and still are), gently encouraging me to step out of thought and into a few precious moments of just being here. If only we could learn that stuff in school!

DEALING WITH THE INNER CRITIC

Many of us live our lives accompanied by an inner voice that is very quick to criticise our failures (and sometimes even our successes), as well as judge the faults and annoying habits of those we spend time with. Some of us tend to put most of the blame for things that go wrong on ourselves, while some of us might blame the rest of the world for our misfortunes. Often our inner voices exaggerate and catastrophise, turning molehills into mountains. At times these inner critics can become toxic.

Whatever your poison, it may well be that when you start to meditate you become even more aware of these tendencies. Over time we can learn to notice, even embrace, these moaning minnies. Learning to not identify our whole selves with these insubstantial but often overbearing thoughts can be highly liberating. To be guided and supported through this process it can be very helpful to join a group led by experienced mindfulness practitioners.

NEXT STEPS

If there is a possibility for you to do a full 8-week mindfulness course locally, I would highly recommend doing so. Taking a course with an experienced instructor and being able to share the journey with others is by far the best way to embark on a mindfulness programme. If you live in a place where attending a group course is not an option for you, there is an excellent online MBSR course from The Center for Mindfulness at the University of Massachusetts Medical School. You can access the course online and do it in your own time (www.umassmed.edu/cfm/mindfulness-based-programs/mbsr-courses).

You could also try doing a self-directed course at home (or with a reading group at school) such as the one mentioned earlier by Mark Williams and Danny Penman: *Mindfulness: A Practical Guide to Finding Peace in a Frantic World* (2011). This course speaks directly to the self-care aspect and is particularly helpful in helping us recognise early symptoms of exhaustion and burnout. It indicates ways to focus more on the things that nourish us and less on those that deplete us. Mark Williams' audios are secure and compassionate guides along this uneven but ultimately highly rewarding path.

> 'Happy teachers will change the world.'

Vietnamese Zen master Thich Nhat Hanh, a leading proponent of mindfulness, uses this quote as the guiding principle for his 'Wake Up Schools' initiative. It makes sense to me that if we are well, happy, in touch with our emotions and able to nourish ourselves, then we can teach in a sustainable way that will deeply impact our students. Teaching is a wonderful vocation. But it can be very demanding, and in some contexts exhausting. Taking care of ourselves so that we can continue to teach well and enjoy teaching is just about the most significant thing we can do. Not just for our own benefit but also because of the impact that we have on children and young people.

WHAT REALLY MATTERS?

- Taking a breath, slowing down.

- Taking care of ourselves through cultivating mindful awareness and self-compassion.

TRY IT OUT!

- Stress response – try tuning in to any familiar responses to stress that might arise over the next few days and especially notice (with an open curiosity if you can muster it) where you experience those stress responses in your body.

- Try using the 7/11 breathing technique (see page 42) if you feel any acute stress or to calm yourself before any interactions or 'performances' that elevate your stress levels.

- Try a short daily sitting meditation:

  - set a timer

  - establish an anchor – body, sounds or breath

  - keep coming back to your sensory anchor when you notice the mind has wandered (It will!).

  See the notes on page 46 for guidance.

- Alternatively, try out an online *guided meditation*. Here is a selection of free downloadable audios from a variety of teachers (it may be more convenient to download them to your phone once you find one you like):

  - Audios from the course book *Mindfulness: A Practical Guide to Finding Peace in a Frantic World* by Mark Williams and Danny Penman (2011), which includes a 13-minute bodyscan. Available at http://rodalebooks.s3.amazonaws.com/mindfulness/index.html

  - Selection of short audios from Bangor University Centre for Mindfulness, including short and long bodyscans and mindful walking. Available at www.bangor.ac.uk/mindfulness/audio/index.php.en.

(Continued)

(Continued)

- o UCSD Centre for Mindfulness offers longer bodyscans. Available at https://health.ucsd.edu/specialties/mindfulness/programs/mbsr/Pages/audio.aspx

- o UCLA Mindful Awareness Research Centre. Available at http://marc.ucla.edu/mindful-meditations

- o There are some free guided sessions called *Take 10* on the Headspace app. Available at www.headspace.com/

- o Monash University, Australia. Free online mindfulness course – Mindfulness for Wellbeing and Peak Performance. Available at http://www.monash.edu/health/mindfulness

FURTHER READING AND RESOURCES

Williams, M. and Penman, D. (2011) *Mindfulness: A Practical Guide to Finding Peace in a Frantic World*. London: Piatkus.

I have found this to be the most practical and helpful introduction to mindfulness.

Sapolsky, R. (2004) *Why Zebras Don't Get Ulcers*. New York: Holt.

If you are interested in learning more about stress and its effect on the body, this is a highly readable and sometimes humorous scientific book by a field and lab biologist.

McGonigal, K. (2013) *How to Make Stress Your Friend*. TEDGlobal. Available at https://www.youtube.com/watch?v=RcGyVTAoXEU&ab_channel=TED

An interesting take on stress, highlighting some of its positive effects.

The Center for Contemplative Mind in Society's *Tree of Contemplative Practices* sets mindfulness in context as one of many branches of contemplative and reflective practices and activities. Available at www.contemplativemind.org/practices/tree.

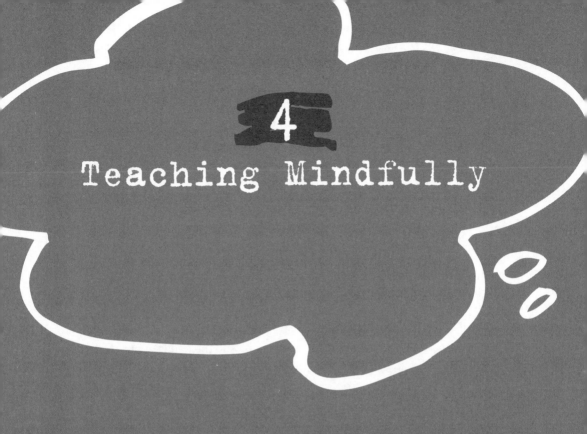

4
Teaching Mindfully

This chapter:

⤳ looks at the value to teachers and students of bringing a more mindful awareness to our teaching

⤳ explores research in social neuroscience concerning the importance of relationship in learning, and the significance of the role of the teacher

⤳ considers how teacher presence can impact both the learning environment and the needs of individual students.

> **Be mindful**
>
> **Teach mindfully**
>
> **Teach mindfulness**

Part 1: Bringing Mindful Awareness into Our Classrooms

Not everyone wants or needs to teach mindfulness to students, but we can all benefit from a training that has the potential to:

- increase our sense of presence

- increase our sensitivity to our own needs and the needs of our students

- heighten our awareness of bodily and emotional cues that guide us in developing this sensitivity.

In short, we can all learn to *teach more mindfully*.

Sometimes concepts like *mindfulness* or *mindfully* can get in the way of our intuitive understanding. No one 'gives us' mindfulness - it's an innate capacity that we can choose to consciously cultivate. In your own teaching you may already have a sense of this but just never actually called it 'mindfulness'. You probably know what it's like when you feel disconnected, detached or distracted - when you *don't* feel you're fully there with the students or the lesson. You probably also know what it's like when you *do* feel present, engaged and really connected with your students. This can include a sense of your own vibrancy when teaching from the front of the class, but it could also be a quieter sense of when the class is working well, of noticing that productive 'buzz' and being able to respond with ease to whatever arises in the moment. This is what I am calling *teaching mindfully*.

LESSONS FROM SOCIAL NEUROSCIENCE

The Social Neuroscience of Education by Louis Cozolino (2013) is an impressive synthesis of a huge amount of research that the author has harvested from the most relevant findings in social neuroscience that relate to the role of the classroom teacher and to optimising the conditions for learning. Cozolino refers to the development of our social brain and our evolutionary history of learning in groups, and from his exploration of the research he concludes that teachers seeking to optimise learning in their classrooms would do well to compare their role with one of a *tribal leader*. Young humans are predisposed, through our child-parent attachment circuitry, to learn in groups from adults who fit this mould. A tribal leader is someone who uses a natural authority that the group senses is directed towards their communal wellbeing. The tribal leader is concerned with protection and with keeping the group safe and healthy. Physical safety is of course essential, but for healthy development and engaged learning group members also need to feel emotionally secure. Good teachers and good leaders provide a sense of a supported safe space in which to learn and grow.

Tribal leaders also aim to find a place and a role for everyone in the group, so embracing and managing diversity is very important to them too. If we want to 'be the best teacher we can be', and to have the deepest impact we can on the students we teach, then acknowledging the importance of these insights from evolutionary science into the power and potential of learning through relationship can help motivate us to continue to connect our personal growth with our professional development.

START WHERE YOU ARE

Some of the most rewarding experiences I have had as a trainer have been with groups of teachers who just wanted to take a course for themselves, to become more mindful, and for this to impact the way they deal with stress and how they teach. To meet these needs we designed a Teaching Mindfully course based on the book *Mindfulness: A Practical Guide to Finding Peace in a Frantic World* (Williams and Penman, 2011) combined with activities and reflections specifically designed for teachers. We will draw from these in this chapter, looking at two key areas that teaching mindfully can influence:

- Optimising learning environments
- Impacting individual students

OPTIMISING LEARNING ENVIRONMENTS

Making Arrangements to be Present

A first step in bringing a more mindful awareness to our teaching is simply to find ways to remember to be more present in the classroom. Here's an exercise adapted from Deborah Schoeberlein's book *Mindful Teaching and Teaching Mindfulness* (2009) that you could try out next week.

 ARRANGING TO BE PRESENT

Pick a class you want to experiment with, or a time of day if you are a primary teacher (or perhaps a regular meeting if you aren't a class teacher) and before you next meet this group familiarise yourself with these steps:

(Continued)

(Continued)

- First, instead of desperately using the final moments before the session begins to reply to some emails or to get some paperwork done or to chat to a colleague, set your intention to be fully prepared before the students arrive.

- Put everything else aside before class starts and take a few moments to calm and ground yourself, perhaps by taking some conscious breaths. Focus on a few full exhales, letting go as best you can.

- Greet the students at the door by looking them in the eye and saying 'Hi' to each of them as they come in. It doesn't really matter how they react, you are just letting them know that you are here and ready.

- Allow the class to settle, take another breath and then just start the class as normal but remain observant and curious about how the next few moments unfold.

- 'Notice what you notice.' As best you can, continue to tune in to your body, thoughts and feelings. Try to be aware of whatever arises; just begin to familiarise yourself with your own reactions and responses in the moment. Try not to be too self-critical.

Checking In

You can try the above exercise for a week or so with the same class/time of day and then, if you want, try finding a way that works for you and for the students to also give *them* a chance to transition from whatever has been happening before they turned up - to give them a chance to fully arrive before you get started. Many teachers naturally use some form of informal check-in, perhaps just having a chat with them about what they've just been doing or about what's coming up for them today. Here are some other ideas you can try, adapting them to suit your classroom needs.

STUDENT CHECK–IN ACTIVITIES

Try this short opener from Susan Kaiser-Greenland (quoted in Willard, 2016).
    Ask each student to complete these two phrases with a word for each (3-5 mins):

'My mind feels ....'

'My body feels ....'

Try to keep it snappy and spontaneous - they don't need to think too much about it; for example, 'My mind feels foggy and my body feels warm', 'My mind feels alert and my body feels sleepy'.

If it's a small group you could go around the room or ask for volunteers. This can help people appreciate the range of mind and body states in the room at any one time, acknowledging that the way we all feel can be different from each other and different for each of us from now to next week, later today or in 10 minutes' time. Next time, when they have the hang of doing this, they could just share in pairs or at a table.

If you prefer, they can simply jot down their two words on Post-it notes on their table and then see if anyone wants to share with the class. Or you could collect them in and read a few out anonymously.

You can also try the same type of exercise as above, but using a different prompt such as 'How's the weather with you today?':

- Just a word or phrase to describe a current mood.

- Establish a 3-5 minute settling routine. This could, for example, be journaling based (see 'Try It Out' at the end of the chapter for examples and resources).

With students that have been trained in mindful awareness, a short shared silence or guided settling can be used instead of, or in conjunction with, these check-ins. (A guided settling is when the teacher leads the students in a short mindfulness practice, similar to the activity we did in Chapter 2, 'Feeling Your Feet'.)

These activities don't have to take long, but if you can get the tone right it can help students be ready to be here and learn with you. I know one teacher who used to tell her secondary students, 'Before we get going today, I just need a moment to settle myself. You can read or sit silently until I'm done. Just don't disturb me. OK?' After a while the majority of the class chose to join her shared silence before each class. For secondary students in particular a simple check-in is also a humane acknowledgement that you know there's more going on for them than just your class.

Here's a different type of check-in that I saw a teacher use effectively at the International School of Prague:

ARTICULATING EMOTIONS

Jason taught special educational needs classes, and one morning I went to do an appraisal observation with him. He was teaching a group of 13-year-old boys and intending to use the class to help them prepare for an algebra test in Maths the next day. The boys sat around a circular table but before starting work they each went over to the side counter and selected two cards that best described how they were feeling from a group of about 50 cut-up and laminated 'emotion words'. Jason did this every Monday with his students to try to get a read on

(Continued)

(Continued)

anything that might be coming up in school for them that week which could need some support from him. The first boy started to read out his words to the group – 'Sad' and 'Upset' – but he only managed to mumble the beginning of a sentence before dissolving into tears and openly sobbing to such an extent that he had to leave the room. Before he left he managed to explain that his new puppy had gone missing the day before and they had not been able to find it. While he went to the bathroom to compose himself Jason did a great job building understanding in the group by asking the other boys if they had ever lost something that really upset them. By the time the boy came back there was a lot of empathy in the room and after a bit they continued to go round the circle and look at each boy's words before starting on the algebra.

I felt a bit sorry for Jason as this all took place in the first moment of the first activity in his first formal observation. But he handled it all very skilfully, and to me this check-in activity and his creation of a safe emotional space for the boys spoke volumes about the value of teachers taking the time to allow for emotional aspects of learning in their classes. If he hadn't done that check-in the boy would probably have held those feelings in all day and the Maths class would probably have produced very little memorable learning for him. (The puppy was found later that afternoon, by the way – didn't want to leave you hanging with that!)

You may feel that with some groups you teach, you would be wary of trying out some of these activities. That's fine. These exercises are more to give you an idea of what it's like when opportunities arise where you might be able to use your mindfulness skills to engage with students on a slightly different level. We don't know at any one time what any of our students might be dealing with and we are not trying to expose children's vulnerability, but we do sometimes need to provide a safe space in case emotions need to surface. The effectiveness of our teaching depends upon the positive emotional engagement of our students and this simple check-in used by a well-attuned teacher who was able to deal appropriately and compassionately with an unexpected situation made all the difference to that child's capacity to learn that day.

Body as Barometer

As we learn to tune in more to our bodies, our feelings and our mental states, we can increase our sensitivity to be able to read physical and emotional cues that may help guide our teaching and make us more effective teachers. As we have noted, mindful awareness training involves consciously connecting with our bodies – noticing our physical aliveness, the physicality of breath and of sensory experiences. In this way we begin to use the body as a barometer – as a way of gauging the climate – or as a radar system giving us early warning of tensions and pressures that, unnoticed, might lead to physical tensions or illness.

As well as promoting better physical and mental health, this increased sensitivity can inform our classroom approach. Understanding our own emotional reactions and triggers helps us develop greater empathic understanding for others, and we can learn to not overreact and not to take things too personally. There are a variety of ways to enhance our sense of classroom presence and our sensitivity in the moment whilst teaching and interacting. The key is developing the ability to notice physical sensations and mental or emotional reactions to what is happening right now. This natural sensitivity can be significantly enhanced through developing a personal mindfulness practice (see Chapter 3). In time this may help us notice subtle triggers and habitual patterns of behaviour that drive our reactions. The more we tune in to the body and use it as an early warning radar system that is giving us information about our subtle reactions to what is happening around us, the more we are able to assess the classroom climate, adjust and make informed decisions about our responses.

TUNING IN

Towards the end of one student mindfulness course, I prepared to take a group of 17-18-year-old high-schoolers on a 'sensory safari' - a walk off campus that would involve silence, deep listening and reflection. Having worked in middle school (11-14 years) for the majority of my teaching career, I don't really see myself as a high-school teacher. As we left the school it began to rain lightly and I stopped the group in a covered alleyway to explain the ground rules for this somewhat unusual learning experience - one that might work against the naturally social grain of the teenage brain. As I stood waiting for the group to assemble I noticed a knot in my belly and an elevated heartbeat. There was a dampness in my palms. A familiar stress signature was beginning to take shape and I took a moment to tune in and turn towards these symptoms. Was I feeling threatened? Yes. Why? Perhaps the body language of the students, my sense that they might not be into this, that I was maybe taking them too far out of their comfort zone? Underlying that, I was aware that I have never really felt that comfortable teaching older adolescents. Perhaps because of my own issues with authority and some deeper rebellious tendencies, perhaps because of my experiences at age 11 when I was in a British grammar school where bullying was the norm. For whatever reasons, my vague fear of not being able to control a group was manifesting itself as threat symptoms in my body.

When we are threatened we close up, our thought processes narrow down towards 'tunnel vision' - not a good state to be in for teaching mindful awareness in nature! So what could I do? All of this happened in the space of a few moments, but the key step had already been taken - by noticing the physical symptoms, and by acknowledging what I was feeling, I was already giving myself some space to manoeuvre with awareness, instead of being subconsciously propelled by my discomfort. Deciding then that a closed response was not where I wanted to be for the next 40 minutes, I was able to internally clarify my intention for the class,

(Continued)

(Continued)

turn a little towards the physical symptoms, take a deeper breath, let go more on the out breath, allow those symptoms to be there ('I don't have to like feeling this way, I just need to accept it'), and then to use this heightened awareness to help guide me into the next moment.

By focusing my alertness onto what I wanted to achieve, onto connecting with the students and internally clarifying my intentions, I was able to avoid overreacting when I saw them not sticking exactly to the ground rules that had been set. Better to have a flexible response, to allow things to settle a little than to sternly force them to behave and be quiet. Acknowledging openly with them that this exercise was unusual - a challenge even - may also have helped the process unfold, whereas clamping down and being strict and demanding might have provoked their own threat or avoidance response which could have cut them off from the sensitive learning experience I was attempting to create for them.

So I gave them some slack as we walked down the hill, not insisting on total silence. Just staying in my own bubble as best I could. Gradually, as we got further away from the buildings and into the trees, they began to quieten until we eventually did have silence and the chance to really appreciate what was around us.

PRESENCE

In training teachers to *teach mindfully* we try to heighten this sensitivity through exercises that enhance our sense of presence in the classroom. These may be activities that increase awareness of body, breath and voice. For example, one of the approaches used by Helle Jensen and Katinka Gøtzsche in training Danish teachers is the *60/40*. In this series of exercises, we play with keeping our attention predominantly in our bodies while moving, breathing and interacting with others. This is good practice for teachers as we are so often caught up in putting 100 per cent of our attention into our teaching and our students that we can forget about ourselves. So here we train to aim to keep roughly 60 per cent awareness inside ourselves and 40 per cent outside.

60/40 MEET 'N GREET (5 MINUTES)

1 Stand up (in your own space as much as possible), bringing attention to sensations in the feet.

2 Notice any tingling, fizzing, temperature.

3 Bend your knees a few times, sensing the weight on the soles of your feet.

4 Very slowly, maintaining awareness of any sensations in the feet, gently lean back and forth, and side to side.

5   Now, maintaining this awareness in the feet, walk around the room and intro-
    duce yourself to someone near you, making sure to shake their hand when
    you do so, still trying to keep about 60 per cent awareness in your feet.

6   Move around again and greet someone else, maintaining awareness in your feet.

(Adapted with permission from a workshop by Katinka Gøtzsche, Aarhus, Denmark,
June 2015)

Like many mindfulness exercises this sounds simple, but it's not easy to maintain
the combination of inner and outer awareness. In many cases, after shaking one
or two people's hands, participants forget that the intention was to keep their
attention on their feet. In discussion after the activity we can reflect on how
easy it is to lose ourselves and on the importance of practice. Setting an intention clearly can help remind us to come back to ourselves from time to time in
the midst of a busy class or day. Otherwise we may end up putting out so much
energy during the day, week or term that we end up drained and exhausted.
Keeping some sense of an inner awareness, on the other hand, helps cue us
to the sensitivities described earlier that may increase the effectiveness of the
learning environment.

Voice training used to be included in initial teacher training in the UK, and considering that the voice is the essential tool of the teacher it makes sense that we
should learn how to take care of it and how to use it to greatest effect. The book
Presence by Patsy Rodenburg (2009) has many activities that help build presence
through breath and voice. Rodenburg mainly trains stage actors but her exercises
work very well for teaching mindfully too. In one of our exercises with teachers
we build up body, breath and voice awareness though a series of activities that
culminate in reading a poem to a small group whilst playing with various aspects
of presence. Before reading or speaking to the group, teachers also look at some
suggestions for areas they can choose to focus on, for example:

- Slowing down
- Breathing
- Speaking mindfully
- Pausing/allowing silence
- Awareness of body
    o   soft gaze - relaxed eyes
    o   allowing oneself to be seen
    o   strong back, tender heart (strong presence yet vulnerable)
- Awareness of emotions
- Awareness of thoughts - softening
- Awareness of environment beyond self.

These suggestions are courtesy of Richard C. Brown, Professor of Contemplative
Education at Naropa University, Boulder, Colorado, USA and come from a longer
unpublished list of 'Contemplative Personal Practices while Teaching' (2014).

TRANSFORMING TEACHING THROUGH MINDFUL AWARENESS

Many teachers in a variety of schools where there is access to mindfulness training for adults have said that they have found this training 'transformational', either personally, professionally or both:

'This course helps you to actively look after your wellbeing. If you are aware of your needs you can be better aware of the needs of your students too.'

'I don't react how I used to when a student pushes my buttons.'

'I'm actually really enjoying connecting with my students these days.'

'It's a practical way for teachers to deal with stress.'

'It is a reminder to seek balance between your job and your professional life which helps to be more effective at your job.'

'It helped me function better as a colleague because it helped me raise my level of awareness for empathy towards others.'

'I was sceptical about this "mindfulness" at first but have found it so helpful.'

'I just feel much calmer.'

Certainly in my personal experience I would agree with all of the above. At a pressured, anxious and difficult stage in my life I began a regular mindfulness practice and after a while I began to notice an impact on how I was at work. I also began to really enjoy teaching my classes to middle school kids. I think what I appreciated more than anything was the fun – and the joy even – that can be found in connecting with students. This was something that over the years I had just lost, or perhaps did not appreciate so much at that time because of other concerns and priorities.

The core of each Teaching Mindfully class is usually spent setting teachers up for one of the home/school practices adapted from *Mindfulness: A Practical Guide to Finding Peace in a Frantic World* (Williams and Penman, 2011). For example, they might be asked to focus on bringing their attention to routine activities and noting physical sensations when, say, drinking a cup of tea or walking around the classroom. They might also be asked to try out some 'habit releasers' to remind themselves to come out of 'auto-pilot' and into presence. This could mean sitting in a different place in meetings, sometimes standing in a different position when teaching, taking a longer breath while the class think about a question you have posed and so on.

Then in the next class we look at what came up for them during the week, anything they might be noticing about themselves and how they are teaching or relating, along with whatever mini-action research we had asked them to explore in the classroom that week. Often, the heightening of self-awareness and sensitivity that these activities and the course-book readings bring will lead to some new observation or insight, and when teachers begin to share these with each other we can mine a rich seam of discoveries that really contribute to deepening mindful teaching.

> 'It's not just the workload, it's the actual drain of having to emotionally hold those 30 individuals in the palm of your hand and getting ready for the next day and then the 30 needy little people are there again – that's where you see the really outstanding teachers are those who have connectedness and genuineness with their class. It doesn't matter so much about teaching style, it's about being genuine and connected.'
>
> Elementary School Principal

We may tend to assume that 'gifted' teachers have a certain innate charisma that engages students in learning, but what we are discovering here is that we can all train to have greater classroom presence – through our physical presence, breath, body and voice awareness and through enhancing our sensitivity to read our own and other people's mind and body states.

RELAXED ALERTNESS

The Yerkes-Dodson principle that was derived in 1908 from experiments with mice and rats demonstrated that an absence of stress can lead to apathy and lethargy whereas too much stress can cause exhaustion and chaos, and that neither extreme is conducive to deep learning.

Not all stress is bad; **eustress** describes a level of stimulation that is beneficial for getting us switched on and motivated to learn (see Figure 4.1). Relevance, responsibility and novelty help prime this state, and when we feel *relaxed and alert* we are in a good space to engage and learn. The word 'alert' actually has its roots in 'alarm', and so there is a connection to fear in the sense of vigilance and wakefulness, but at low levels the impact is positive. If we can find, in our teaching, that sweet spot of relaxed alertness where students feel safe and comfortable

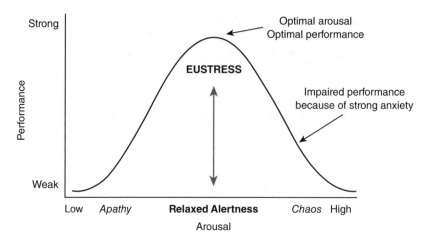

Figure 4.1 Stress and performance (adapted from Diamond et al., 2007)

(but not sluggishly comfortable) and where they are challenged (but not overly challenged), then we can truly optimise learning.

Mindful awareness training is fundamentally a training in relaxed alertness, and as we begin to have a feel for it we can use our own relaxed alertness to influence the classroom environment. As we increase our responsiveness and build emotional safety in our classrooms, we can more consciously create and adapt the quality of the environment to fit the fluctuating needs of the learning focus and of the group. Through noticing subtle cues from within – and from students – we can adjust our pedagogy and fine-tune the atmosphere, creating conditions that come closer to what we understand to be an optimal environment for learning.

Amy Footman, Head of Stanley Grove Primary School in Manchester, talks about how some of her teachers who are trained in mindfulness say they feel 'much more connected with their classes and they talk about how mindfulness makes you more receptive as a teacher instead of being totally caught up in whatever's going on all the time'. And they talk about the idea of 'reading the room': 'Oh, it feels really fizzy in here today, class' or 'I think the classroom feels really, really sleepy today – maybe that's because our minds and bodies are needing a bit more energy.'

Having consciously identified the mood, atmosphere or energy levels of a class, teachers can then adapt their tone, approach or activities accordingly. They might decide to select a short activity designed to calm students down or wake them up as necessary. These could, for example, be simple mindful movement exercises – slow and gentle, or quick and energising (*gear shifting* activities, as the Danish teacher trainers call them), followed by a calm noticing moment when students tune in to the body, observing how it feels, before continuing with the lesson. (For some examples of simple 'activities to calm or energise' a class, see 'Try It Out' at the end of the chapter.)

I have heard from teachers in many schools that taking an 8-week mindfulness course has transformed their experience at home and in the classroom. Enhanced emotional regulation is often referred to in some form or other. Tracy (not her real name) was not someone her colleagues could imagine getting into mindfulness, but she did take a course, not intending to teach students but for her own benefit: 'It's changed my life,' she told me, 'I used to get so easily triggered by certain behaviours in my students, but now it seems like I can notice it, notice my reactions and make choices about how I want to be. I just don't react like I used to.'

IMPACTING INDIVIDUAL STUDENTS

We are above all social beings, and whilst the traditional theory of evolutionary development is based upon the survival of competing species, human achievement may be far more dependent on our ability to collaborate. In pulling together a wealth of research from social neuroscience, Louis Cozolino (2013) points educators to some valuable implications arising from our growing understanding of the science of relationship.

Our Capacity for Attachment

Our brain has evolved to enable us to act collaboratively and collectively and to develop the communication and linguistic skills that have enabled our extraordinary development as a species. In our early stages we are totally dependent on our care-givers and this close, dependent, *attachment* underlies our capacity to learn. As well as providing physical safety and nourishment, our parents regulate our emotions and provide a gateway to learning the literacies upon which our full functionality in culture and society depend.

Although human babies are born without a developed prefrontal cortex and are, for many years, highly dependent and vulnerable offspring, we are also born with some highly developed capacities. The ability of a young baby to 'read' a whole range of facial expressions that convey important social messages is a highly sophisticated form of literacy. The progression from reading faces to becoming literate in understanding and producing complex sounds, then going on to being able to read and write complex language systems, is what ultimately enables us to think abstractly, to reflect and to explore our inner selves and the outer universe.

Relationship in Learning

Although most of our initial communication as infants is non-verbal, on a basic and daily level we grow to communicate with each other through words and ideas, as well as through touch and emotions. Our evolutionary tendency is to learn best when engaged in communication with others in ways that contain this affective component (Marzano et al., 2011: 5-7). As Cozolino shows through the depth of research in the field of attachment theory and human learning, it is here that the potential and power of the role of the teacher is situated. Because of our evolutionary predisposition to connect with our adult care-givers, and the neuroscientific processes that provide this functionality, we are also predisposed to enter into learning relationships with other adults in our community - and in our current version of community that means, for the most part, with our teachers. (After all, in many communities, if you look at the time children spend interacting with adults, a significant chunk of that is spent with their teachers.)

Neuro–Scientific Sculptors

What is most fascinating in reading the research in this area is that scientists can now track the underlying mechanisms of this 'learning through relationship' at a cellular level. On the one hand, none of this is new to us. We know instinctively and through our own relationships and experience what has helped us to grow, develop and learn. But on the other hand, we can also begin to understand and actually 'see' through brain research the intricacies of the physiology of learning and relationship. So much so that, based on this evidence, Cozolino describes teachers as *neuro-scientific sculptors* who, by means of their personal and pedagogical capacities, create learning environments and internal connections in their students that literally 'sculpt' the synaptic frameworks of our brains. How cool is that!

Life Lesson No. 1

Deeper still, when we look at the crucial importance of early attachment in the life of a young human, we can begin to understand how we might grow up lacking some key social and emotional skills - especially if our primary care-givers were unable to meet some of our needs or to engage fully in our early development. Primary care-givers regulate our early emotional responses and if they are themselves missing some key capacities, then the gaps in the attunement between children and parents can, in later life, cause significant problems in our personal and professional relationships. Developmentally appropriate programmes and approaches that give young students the time and space to explore social and emotional skills can perhaps help fill some of those gaps.

Younger children do not have fully developed cognitive capacities, but this is a fertile time for the natural development of the affective skills. Well-attuned children will naturally know if their mum is angry, or even have a fair sense of whether a stranger is to be trusted or not. Quality social and emotional learning (SEL) programmes that help develop these skills can heighten and enhance our abilities so that we can, for example, learn to be more empathetic even when in conflict, and can train to be less judgmental and more compassionate to ourselves and others. These programmes need to be more than just cleverly designed 'academic' programmes: they need to have authentic experiential components and, most importantly, they need to be taught by people who can embody the qualities sought.

Life Lesson No. 2

In addition to the need for the conscious development of social and emotional skills through well-taught formal and informal programmes, there is another important finding arising from research on attachment that is highly relevant to teachers. This is the impact through modelling and connection that a significant adult can have on an insecure child who has deficits in social skills or emotional regulation.

Our students are registering all sorts of messages in a classroom environment besides the content of the class that we are so focused on imparting. These include the body language of the teacher and of peers, sensitivities to humorous or threatening behaviours, group dynamics that can bolster or threaten self-esteem and status and so on. How the adult in the room holds himself or herself in relation to the class, and to potential threats to social and emotional stability, are keenly noted. Difficult student behaviour can easily trigger our own hotspots and deficits in relationship skills or in handling confrontation. Bringing a more mindful awareness to our reactions can help us develop the capacity to choose appropriate responses to challenging situations.

'Teach Your Children Well'

As well as improving our behaviour management skills we are also providing opportunities for individual students to learn from us through witnessing responses that might contradict, or throw into question, their early modelling patterns. Something as simple as seeing you not take anger personally can be profound for a child who has not witnessed that at home. A child in your class may have learned to use defensive aggression to mask a subconsciously felt inadequacy. If they surface hostility in an interaction with you but you don't react to it and are able to maintain a kind but firm demeanour, along with a patient curiosity in your interactions, this could teach them a life lesson that they have not yet had a chance to learn. Likewise a teacher who communicates (directly or indirectly) that they have the patience to stick with a student and to support them even if they may feel hopeless at something can help that individual learn a powerful lesson that might stay with them throughout their life.

> I've come to a frightening conclusion that I am the decisive element in the class-room. It's my personal approach that creates the climate. It's my daily mood that makes the weather. As a teacher, I possess a tremendous power to make a child's life miserable or joyous ... I can humiliate or heal. In all situations, it is my response that decides whether a crisis will be escalated or de-escalated and a child humanized or dehumanized. (Ginott, 1994 [1972])

This may all sound a bit intense or overwhelming to you as a teacher with so much else on your mind: 'I have enough to do getting through the day and delivering the History curriculum to 30 disparate individuals in each of my five classes – I don't have time to be a therapist as well!'

True. But these indications from social neuroscience research should not be taken to imply that we need to be perfect human beings able to solve every child's problems. It's more about being human despite our imperfections, and being aware of the impact we might have on children.

Re-attunement: Ian Wright meets Mr Pigden

If you can, take 3 minutes to watch the video about Ian Wright, a famous English football player. Having retired from football he now works on radio and television, and this video was taken while he was filming another programme. Without his knowledge the director had contacted Wright's primary school teacher, not realis-ing quite what impact this would have on the famous sportsman.

Ian Wright gets a big shock!:

www.youtube.com/watch?v=omPdemwaNzQ&ab_channel=MITOGEN

In other programmes Ian Wright has talked about his difficult upbringing, and we can see the wonderful impact Mr Pigden has had on him. It's quite extraordinary to see how this grown man, an accomplished athlete, reverts, in front of the camera, to a young child, respectfully taking off his cap and movingly holding his teacher's hand. Wright had a very tough childhood which resulted in him carrying a lot of anger and easily getting into uncontrollable rages. He says that Mr Pigden took the time to teach him how to communicate with others and was his first positive male role model and the one who made him feel important and capable.

If you listen to people talk about an important person in their life other than their parents or partner, you often hear them describe a key characteristic that this person had: 'He was so patient', 'Such a calm person', 'She was so enthusiastic about her sub-ject', 'So caring' and so on. These people are seeing a quality in someone – quite often their teacher – that they had lacked in their own upbringing and so in themselves. Sometimes people who grow up having experienced insecure early attachments might only need to have a positive relationship with one other significant person who is secure in themselves to kick-start some of these missing qualities.

This process of 're-attunement' builds on the neurobiological circuitry that helps us attune and attach to our early caregivers (for further details, see Cozolino, 2013: 18, 106–107). There are many accounts of this sort of learning relationship having a profound impact on people for the rest of their lives. It doesn't have to be when you are a child – some people talk about university or college professors who have had a similar impact on them. It doesn't necessarily have to be a teacher, of course, it can be a relationship with a partner or other significant adult, but teachers are often cited because they are working in a context where re-attunement with a secure adult is a distinct possibility. Re-attunement does not only happen to people who have suffered abuse or serious lack in childhood – we are all stronger in some areas of social and emotional development and weaker in others, so all students can benefit from authentic connection with their teachers, as well as, and ideally in combination with, well-designed, well-taught social-emotional skills programmes.

Our human physiology has such strong social and emotional foundations, and teaching is such a social profession, that we can all benefit from paying attention to our social and emotional growth and wellbeing. On some level, you may never know the impact you have had on the children you have taught, both in terms of subject learning and in terms of other life skills they might have picked up along the way. But we can celebrate the opportunity to be involved in such potentially powerful learning relationships and also re-commit to doing the best we can to further the growth of the individuals and groups we teach.

Shifting our focus to our own affective skills can enable us to teach more mindfully. This in turn can help us teach more effectively and support our wellbeing by taking better care of ourselves and our students. We now have the evidence and understanding available to guide teachers much more effectively in this area. In many ways, *teaching mindfully* is an act of self-care itself, and it's important that schools help us foster this crucial capacity to take care of ourselves. Schools and educational institutions can do this by making training in self-care a normal part of professional development and initial teacher training. In Part 2 of this chapter we look more directly at this question of preparation in initial teacher training.

Part 2: Mindfulness and Relational Competence in Teacher Training

> Many teachers and student teachers see relations and interaction with the students as the most difficult aspect of teaching, and they experience that their teacher training does not prepare them sufficiently for these aspects of the teaching profession. (Jensen et al., 2015)

This statement comes from an interim report of a Danish research study entitled 'Educating teachers focusing on the development of reflective and relational competences'. This Danish study, described in some detail below, gives us an insight into the kind of practical preparation for a career in teaching that a focus on our own social and emotional skills can provide.

WHEN DID YOU NOTICE YOU HAD LOST YOURSELF?

Mindfulness and Relational Competence Training for Trainee Teachers

Aarhus University and VIA University College, Denmark

'There is a need for student teachers to learn about and to develop relational competence during their teacher education programme in order to be able to create and maintain good-quality teacher–student relations, which provide the basis for a high-quality learning environment in which pupils can learn and thrive.'

In 2015 at a conference in Denmark, my wife and I met three remarkable ladies who are part of a larger group collaborating on research in training for teachers in what the Danes call 'Relational Competence'.

A 2008 review of 220 studies of different factors of importance for the learning environment by the Danish Pedagogical University concluded that 'If we want to create a good learning environment it´s important to teach teachers to create good relations: To show tolerance, respect, interest, empathy and compassion to each child.' This research project in Aarhus is one of several efforts to explore precisely what makes for an effective training of relationship skills for teachers.

The current research project (2012–2016 and beyond) grew out of an earlier study on the impact of teaching mindfulness and contemplative practices to 11–13-year-old students in an ordinary school. In this first study the children described how they had experienced the mindfulness training. One 13-year-old boy said, 'Usually you are very busy in the morning and you have to run out to get to school and then you are stressed at the end of school, but when we do these exercises in the morning it's as if the stress crawls out of your body and you get relaxed ready to learn.'

Professor Anne Maj Nielsen, Head of Educational Psychology Department at the Danish School of Education at Aarhus University, said, 'One thing we learned from the part of this first study that followed the teachers was that it is very important to have a mutual context in which to practice mindfulness. Meditative practices are very difficult to keep up on your own – especially for busy teachers. So we realised we needed to include this as part of teacher education. By incorporating this into an initial teacher training degree, we would have the opportunity to offer a kind of social anchor to practice – to have it become habituated as part of your everyday life.'

Taking the training to the VIA University College, a teacher training school in Aarhus, the researchers tracked student teachers over the 4 years of their Bachelor of Education course. The trainee teachers in the trial group were regularly interviewed and they tried to describe what it is like for them on occasions when they feel they are able to be a good teacher – how they were aware of themselves and aware of what was going on with their students. They also described their experiences when things were not going well, when they were *not* able to be aware – or when they became aware of what was going on just after an incident.

For example, a male teacher felt provoked by a child so he told the student to leave the classroom. Then he felt ashamed that he had done that because it didn't really solve the problem so then he told the rest of the class, 'Wait a moment I need to go talk to that student because I want him to stay in the class.'

The difficult part of that process was for the student teacher to admit to himself that it was a bad choice to ask the student to leave. But then he found the space to think, 'OK, this is what I need to do to take care of the relationship with the boy and with the class.'

'One thing that is common to the student teachers in the group,' Professor Neilsen suggests, 'is the ability to be more aware of their own state of mind and their own emotions and their own impulses to react. To be aware of it and not just to act on it. To be aware of it as it happens and at the same time to be aware of what is going on with the students they are teaching.'

This enhanced sensitivity has enabled trainee teachers to step back, develop greater empathy and broaden their perspective – they talked about how you can understand the student either as someone who wants to provoke you, or as a child who doesn't really understand what is going on, or as just a child who is having fun, even if it is annoying you.

Professor Nielsen explains, 'If you are able to see a child as a vulnerable person for whom it's hard to learn, or perhaps as someone who is afraid to make mistakes that could lead to ridicule, then as a teacher it's important to take care of dealing with mistakes and with how you might make the child feel in the classroom.'

In another situation a student teacher described how she managed to stop herself from over-reacting – by becoming aware that she was not breathing properly and noticing that she was getting very annoyed and then deciding to take a deep breath. This gave her the space to reframe her view of the student who seconds ago had been experienced as a provocative child – 'Maybe that could have been me a few years ago.'

'This training on Relational Competence only accounted for 5 per cent of their studies at VIA,' said Professor Nielsen, "but it has made a very big impact.'

Katinka Gøtzsche is a co-trainer for the student teachers and a secondary school teacher herself. 'For me as a teacher, this training has helped me to wait a little in challenging situations. It's not that it takes away the emotions – I can still get very irritated and annoyed – but it helps me to not react and to keep the feelings to myself and not react on my students. I think in the long term it's very helpful for teachers and I guess it makes you more resilient somehow.'

'When our student teachers started teaching they realised it actually had a great impact, that it was very important and that it helped them to be better teachers. Also, as a teacher, just to take some pauses in your teaching. "How do I feel now? What is this doing to me as a teacher?" The children don't have to know about it. You just need your awareness, "OK, I see I'm getting annoyed now."'

Helle Jensen, a psychologist, family therapist and lead trainer on the project, describes the courses they gave the student teachers as training in 'Relational Competence, Empathy and Presence'. 'Most of the student teachers – who were all chosen randomly – didn't want the training at first, but I think they realised it had a great impact on their way of dealing with classroom challenges and with parents.'

(Continued)

(Continued)

'We started the course by looking first at themselves as part of their own personal professional development. Learning about how your own way of being is influencing the learning environment in the classroom. This was very different for them. "We didn't come here to talk about ourselves, we came to learn how to teach children!" Some were quite furious at the beginning. Over time I think the mindfulness exercises helped them come to the point of seeing themselves as part of the problem. They could begin to see themselves as the ones who can create a problem, or solve a problem.

The trainees in the trial group were filmed on their teaching practices and they learnt to reflect openly on any challenging situations they had encountered with a trainer and their peers. Jensen believes it's this reflection that often brings the greatest learning and that helps develop more mindful teaching.

'They have to talk about what makes a good learning environment. This is part of the training, not only developing the mindful awareness but also how to put into words what happened in this little sequence. The point where something essential happened. They learn to identify this point, "When did I first lose myself in this interaction?", "Could I have done something else at that point?" This is easier to identify if you do mindfulness exercises.'

From observing the growth of the trainee teachers and from their feedback, Jensen concludes that one of the key tools the students have picked up from the training is how to be able to work with their attitude and mood. They know, for example, that the way you enter the classroom is significant, and it impacts the way the learning will unfold. They also know they can change their attitude.

'We teach them a 3-minute exercise, one the teacher can do before they go into the classroom. You learn to quickly get in touch with body, heart, breathing, and mental state to see how each is right now.'

In one case, a trainee was working with a group of 14-year-old boys. He liked the boys but when they were together they would never listen and he found he got annoyed with them. In reviewing this later with his peers he was asked a series of questions:

'How does it feel for you when you revisit this now, a situation that didn't go well?'

'What were you feeling in your body?'

'How was your empathy for yourself and for them?'

'How was your ability to focus or to think clearly? Did you have ideas of how to get out of the situation?'

'This way of changing his own attitude can help the student. No one gave him any solutions, but it became clear to him that before he went into the next class, he could take the 3 minutes to acknowledge his state, to be more conscious about his emotions – to take responsibility for how he is feeling right now.

Owning our own emotions is very important – otherwise these feelings are 'homeless' – and when you take them into the class, they will get expressed in ways that are not helpful. If the boys feel bad or that it's them that are in the wrong they will do things to get rid of this bad feeling.'

'It's important to have this dialogue with yourself and with others because we need help to gain clarity about how things are. You have to express it, to name it. When we express ourselves and then get in touch with our natural competencies we don't need to know a lot about theory we just need to be interested and listen to ourselves.'

So this training revolves around using the competencies to bring us back to a more authentic, empathic state and then around remembering to use these in the moment. The student teachers learn to take mini-pauses for themselves, to check-in from time to time and in addition they learn short 'gear shifting' activities they can use with children to change the energy in a classroom.

The research study is ongoing but the preliminary report after the first 18 months found that, compared with a control group, the student teachers in the trial were:

- more active and reflective in establishing relations with students in school;

- more reflective and experimental in relation to their teacher role.

Student teacher:

'In the project I learned to pay attention to how I enter the teacher role. It is important ... to balance between being professional and at the same time just stick to being myself.

Professor Nielsen:

'Through noticing their inner impulses as well as external factors it makes it possible for the teachers to become aware of what is going on and to keep in mind that they are able to still be the adult in the room or still be the one to take care of the situation – including taking care of themselves.'

A NEW TEACHER'S PERSPECTIVE

I've tried to not push mindfulness with my children, concerned that they might just see it as 'Dad's thing' (or perhaps 'Dad's really weird thing') and of causing an adverse reaction. But I was thrilled to hear recently that my eldest daughter, now in her second year of primary school teaching in Scotland, is doing a mindful awareness training course for herself – provided free to teachers in her area by the education authority (Hooray!). Knowing the significant demands on young teachers in the education system and the limited focus on equipping them with affective self-management skills on teacher training courses, I was really pleased to hear that she has the opportunity at this stage in her career to learn some fundamental stress management techniques. This could help guide her towards greater self-care and also ultimately might enable her to begin to share this work directly and indirectly with her students.

Here's what Lucy herself says about mindfulness and teacher training:

HOW MINDFULNESS HELPED ME

While doing my own mindfulness training I have been reflecting on times when I've had a bad day and tried really hard to not let that affect the kids. I noticed that it's really hard to do!

The Introduction to Mindfulness course, though, has helped me in:

- being able to notice when my stress levels are getting to a point of no return. It's both a physical thing – heart beating really fast, almost hyperventilating, almost crying (or crying!) – and it's also mental – recognising where my thoughts have gone

- being able to stop before I get really worked up and letting it go for a bit

- being compassionate to myself, when you feel like you are not good enough – – 'It's okay', 'I'm okay'

- learning to appreciate the kids more.

I was so lucky that I was doing mindfulness training at a time in my first year at this school when I had to deal with some really difficult situations.

At teachers' college you are constantly being told that 'You will need to take care of yourself because it's very, very stressful.' But they don't teach you any coping strategies. You want practical things that you can apply when you are teaching.

What you get with mindfulness is something that is going to help you cope.

It would be especially good to have an introduction to mindfulness in the teacher trainee year because that's a very stressful time itself – even before you are a teacher on your own – and then you will already have some of those skills to use on the teacher training and then to use after you graduate and start teaching.'

I wish in teacher training I had learned about:

- Thinking about how you as a person can affect the children you are teaching.

- The importance of being aware of your emotional state and your stress levels. You never think about how that's going to affect the children. You do a lot of work with the kids to name their emotions and so on but don't really bring that to yourself.

- Coping strategies – take a breath, take a moment.

- Your body as barometer – it would have been amazing to know that early on.

Lucy Hawkins, Primary School Teacher, UK

Here are a few statements from other teachers highlighting 'Things I wish I had learned in teacher's training':

- How to deal with stress during the busy times: report writing, conferences.
- How to manage my own emotions, especially when students – or parents or other colleagues – push my buttons.
- How to manage my workload.
- Ways to cope with the emotional unrest that I can feel when teaching students in difficult situations.
- How to deal with difficult parents.
- That the relationship I build with students is a form of classroom management.
- Understanding a student's emotional situation and how this can affect their learning.
- That academic and social and emotional wellbeing are not separate entities.
- How to refuel when you have given so much of yourself emotionally.
- That teaching can be draining but you can recharge with silence and solitude – that you can respect that about yourself and surround yourself with others who respect self-knowledge.
- That the way I am when I teach can have positive (and negative) outcomes on my students' learning.
- To be myself in the classroom, not to try to be an 'idea' of what I think a teacher should be.
- That creating a positive relationship with my student's *is* classroom management.
- How to be nice to myself.

When I was in teacher's college, I remember that one of my professors said that teachers have the highest rate of bladder infections of any other profession, which she seemed to think was pretty funny. She went on to say it's because teachers don't go to the bathroom as often as they should because they are too busy teaching or running around before and after class trying to get things done. She seemed totally okay with this. I was not okay with this! She also briefly mentioned that, as future teachers, we are really going to need to look after ourselves because it's a very stressful job. But there was never any information about *how* to do this. No practical tips, no advice. For me, mindfulness was one of the tools I used to help with my own stress management. It has helped me to be more aware of my body and its needs. So if I'm at school and my body tells me that it needs to go to the bathroom, I listen to it! I can't be present for my students and attentive to their needs if I am not attentive to my own.

High School Guidance Counsellor, Canada

I kept thinking about where to place mindfulness training and I thought, 'It needs to be in teacher training'. If it could be put in a module in teacher training courses, that would be the most effective and beneficial place for potential teachers to learn the techniques both for themselves and for their future students. This is an approach that can promote creativity for teachers as well as to help manage the workload. I wish I had learned some of those skills early in my teaching career. Even a slight change in the way that a teacher relates to a child can make a massive difference to their school experience.

Liz Lord, Special Educational Needs Coordinator, UK

CARE' Program Research

Although mindful awareness training for teachers is still quite new, we are beginning to see various types of evidence, not just anecdotal, of the impact of undergoing this type of training on teaching and learning. A recent study (Jennings et al., 2015) tested the efficacy of the CARE training (Cultivating Awareness and Resilience in Education) on primary school teachers. This large-scale randomised control study followed over 200 teachers in 36 urban elementary schools in New York. As well as a large range of quantitative and qualitative research approaches, the study looked at the impact on students, using observers in every classroom before and after the 8-week training course. As well as significant positive effects of the training compared with the control groups in terms of teachers' emotional regulation, sense of time pressure and stress symptoms, the report showed a clear impact in the classroom on the emotional support aspect for students, as well as improved classroom organisation. The report concluded that,

> These findings have promising implications for education policy because they demonstrate that learning environments can be improved by supporting teachers' social and emotional competence.

COURSES FOR TEACHER SELF–CARE AND TEACHING MINDFULLY

SMART (Stress Management and Relaxation Techniques in Education)

SmartEducation™ is an evidence-based programme that specifically targets the needs of K-12 educators and professional support staff, with a strong emphasis on the cultivation of mindful awareness including elements of self-compassion, emotional literacy, self-regulation skills, optimism and self-care. The SmartEducation™ programme involves experiential activities in mindfulness, including meditation, emotional awareness and movement.

CARE for Teachers (Cultivating Awareness and Resilience in Education)

CARE for Teachers is a programme designed to help teachers reduce stress and enliven their teaching by promoting awareness, presence, compassion, and reflection. Training in relaxation, movement and deep listening can strengthen the inner resources needed to help students flourish, socially, emotionally and academically.

For further information go to www.care4teachers.com.

WHAT REALLY MATTERS?

- Teachers!
- The quality of our relationships with our students.
- *How* we teach is as important as *what* we teach.

TRY IT OUT!

For yourself:

- *Personal practice*: continue to work towards a daily sit, using the ideas and audios from Chapter 3 to support you.
- Try the Making Arrangements to Be Present exercise on page 55.
- Focus on one class and go through the checklist each time before you meet them.

With your students:

- In the following week, you could try out one or more of the student 'Check-in' activities on page 56.
- Try this with the same class as above.

(Continued)

(Continued)

- You can also use 'student journaling prompts' for brief writing exercises as settling routines, eg:

  o Which is louder a frown or a smile? Explain why.

  o Do you feel like you can control your emotions or do your emotions control you? Explain using a specific example.

  o What is your favourite day of the week? Why?

  o List 8-10 things that you are thankful for.

  o What kind of 'thought attack' do you get most often? In other words, what do you worry about? How do you deal with this worrying?

  o Do you show compassion towards yourself or are you hard on yourself? Explain using specific examples.

  o Can you think of a time when your gut/intuition influenced your decision?

- Make up your own, perhaps adapted to your teaching area, or find great journal ideas at https://daringtolivefully.com/journal-prompts

  o Doodling, drawing or colouring – this can be a fun and absorbing alternative, and you can print free designs from https://printmandala.com/.

- Explore working with the energy and atmosphere of a class:

  o Notice fluctuations in attention, engagement, group mood.

  o Tune in to your body to note any subtle cues, tensions, positive sensations.

  o Use your voice, body breaks, short shared silences or listening practices to soften or sharpen attention, to energise when sluggish or to calm when hyper.

SHORT EXERCISES TO CALM OR ENERGISE A CLASS

These activities can ease transitions and also help get us out of thought mode and more connected with the body. We have used these with all age groups, including adults. It's important when you lead these that you too participate. *Even the Energisers can become Calming activities if you follow them with a quiet moment of standing and noticing the effect on the body, before moving on.*

HANDS SHAKE - ENERGISER! (2 MINS)

1. Invite your students to stand up, knees slightly bent, bounce up and down gently a few times feeling your feet connected to the ground.

2. Start shaking the hands, gently at first.

3. Then shake harder.

4. Then shake as hard as you can (being aware of your neighbour and any jewellery you might be wearing) as you count down from 10 out loud. You can play with the pace of the count, encouraging your students to shake faster and harder (within reason!).

5. When you get to 0, invite them to all stop, a let the arms hang, tuning in to any sensations they feel in their hands, their arms, the rest of their body.

6. Perhaps invite them to pair share/whole group share about what they notice.

Note: a few minutes later you can invite students to connect back to their hands, even without moving.

BODY WIGGLE – ENERGISER! (4 MINUTES)

1. Invite your students to stand up, knees slightly bent, bounce up and down gently a few times feeling your feet connected to the ground.

2. Invite them to move their little fingers in circles, then the ring fingers, next fingers and so on, tuning into the sensations of the small circles. Then include the wrists and from here on, keep all of the parts of the body moving as you include others – elbows, arms, ankles (one then the other), knees, hips, neck, and torso until as many body parts as possible are making circles at the same time

Note: it's impossible to keep it all going, which is part of the fun!

3. Then invite them to stop, tune into the sensations in their body. Maintain awareness of the sensations as the students move back to their seats.

SHAKE LIKE A WET DOG – ENERGISER! (1 MINUTE)

1. Pretty self-explanatory! Start with a slow body shake and build up to shaking like a wet dog.

Note: you can show a video of a dog doing this to get them in the mood.

EYES AND EARS – CALMING (2-4 MINUTES)

1. Invite students to rub the palm of their hands together.

2. Generate some heat if possible.

3. Place hands gently over the eyes, palms cupping the eyes.

4. Tune into any sensations.

5. Repeat.

6. Rub hands together, cup around the ears, then gently pinch ears giving them 'mini-hugs.'

(Continued)

(Continued)

FINGER PRESS - CALMING (2-4 MINUTES)

1. Invite students to place their hands on the desk, palms down.

2. Slowly press the left little finger into the desk, release. Encourage them to do this so no one would be able to tell that they are pressing. Continue with the next finger as you move through each on one hand and then the other.

3. After you have led the class through one 'pass,' invite them to do it at their own pace. When finished they can work on pressing down the whole hand at once, again, with the intention that no one would be able to tell that they are pressing.

TAPPING - ENERGISER! (2-5 MINUTES)

1. Invite your students to stand up, knees slightly bent, bounce up and down gently a few times feeling your feet connected to the ground.

2. Taking the tips of your fingers, start *gently* tapping the head, all around, including the top, sides, hairline.

3. Gently move to tapping the face, forehead, cheeks, nose, jaw.

4. Then using palms or fists, start patting the chest.

5. Then move down one arm, then up the same arm. Repeat on the other side.

6. Before moving to the abdomen, remind students to be gentle as the organs are a little more sensitive here.

7. Stronger fists can pat the hips simultaneously.

8. Use both hands to move down the front of one leg, then up the back of the same leg. Repeat on the other side.

9. Gently tap lower back/kidneys.

10. End with patting hands together = applause!

CLOCKWISE CHALLENGE - CALMING AND ENERGISING! (3 MINUTES)

1. Invite your students to stand up, knees slightly bent, bounce up and down gently a few times feeling your feet connected to the ground.

2. Lean weight onto left leg, raise right knee up and start making clockwise circles with the lower leg. If you need to hold something with the left hand to stay balanced, no problem.

3. Establish this focus and balance then introduce the next instruction.

4. The challenge is to continue the clockwise circles with the right lower leg while, at the same time taking the right hand and 'drawing' the number 6 in the air with the index finger. For some reason, this seems impossible to do!

FURTHER READING AND RESOURCES

Cozolino, L. (2013) *The Social Neuroscience of Education: Optimizing Attachment and Learning in the Classroom*. New York: Norton.

A highly impressive gathering and analysis of a body of research that has significant implications for how we teach.

Weaver, L. and Wilding, M. (2013) *The Five Dimensions of Engaged Teaching: A Practical Guide for Educators*. Bloomington, IN: Solution Tree Press.

A rare and highly practical professional development manual for teachers that is based on self-care, mindfulness and emotional intelligence.

Marzano, R.J. and Pickering, D.J. with Heflebower, T. (2011) *The Highly Engaged Classroom*. Bloomington, IN: Marzano Research Laboratory.

Robert Marzano is widely respected for his research and evidence-based publications and this one applied to building student attention and engagement contains classroom examples and ideas as well as the theory that supports them.

Powell, K. and Kusuma-Powell, O. (2010) *Becoming an Emotionally Intelligent Teacher*. London: Corwin.

A valuable practical guide to increasing affective skills and improving relationships in the classroom:

'While teachers do not have absolute control over the emotional weather of the classroom, they have a powerful influence over the affective climate. More often than not, their verbal and nonverbal behaviours and their displays of emotion, dispositions and moods can have powerful effects upon their students. The emotions that teachers display – both consciously and unconsciously – can significantly enhance or inhibit student learning.'

Rodenburg, P. (2009) *Presence: How to Use Positive Energy for Success in Every Situation*. London: Penguin.

Rodenberg's idea of 1st, 2nd and 3rd circles of presence and interaction is particularly helpful for teachers (as well as her normal target audience: actors).

5
Teaching Mindfulness

This chapter:

⤳ looks at how mindful awareness training is being used with students in schools to build attention skills, empathy and compassion

⤳ examines research that supports the use of mindfulness in education

⤳ shows how students apply the training to increase focus, regulate emotions and manage stress.

> **Be mindful**
>
> **Teach mindfully**
>
> **Teach mindfulness**

THE WHOLE CHILD

My own passion for bringing mindful awareness training to children and teachers stems from two key experiences: one was the introduction to meditation I received courtesy of an impromptu overland trip to India in the 1970s; the other was a difficult period I experienced in midlife, when I came to rediscover meditation and mindfulness out of necessity to help me cope and support myself. The training I did then helped me with some basic life skills that I wish I had learnt when I was 15 instead of 50. The effect was so significant and positive that when I emerged from this dark period I looked around for ways to bring some training in this area to the students in my school in Prague. It just seemed to make sense that many young people would benefit from an introduction to mindfulness.

This shift may not, though, at first sight, be an obvious one for schools to make. Mainstream education often prioritises academic, analytical and competitive skills above social, emotional and collaborative competencies. The narrow focus that predominates in many schools reflects an imbalance in the wider world. But if we really want to help young people develop into balanced adults who can engage creatively with the complex issues that are currently challenging us as a species, then we need to begin to shift the focus of schooling to cultivate the full range of our human capacities.

For schools to develop 'the whole child' we need to 'incorporate' (literally 'bring into the body') holistic approaches that combine academic skills more explicitly with the social, emotional and physical aspects of being human. Although all learning depends on the effective use of the mind, few school systems teach students directly about how the mind works and about the integrated nature of mind, heart and body systems.

COMPELLED TO TEACH

Many of us have a 'compulsion to teach' and I remember once being on a silent retreat in Devon in England and stumbling upon what felt like some quite powerful personal insights during the meditation sessions. In my one-to-one with the retreat leader I told her about my experiences and about how I thought I could apply them to teaching mindfulness to students and teachers in my school. 'Hang on a minute Kevin,' she responded, 'There needs to be at least a brief moment between having these insights for your own growth and trying to use them with others in your work.' Caught out!

There's nothing wrong with having this 'compulsion to teach' - it's what brings many of us into teaching, and it may also be what initially motivates many teachers to engage in mindful awareness training. That's fine, but the potential impact of this work relies on our ability to deepen our own personal understanding and self-awareness.

NOT YOUR AVERAGE PROFESSIONAL DEVELOPMENT

If you intend to teach mindfulness to students, it's good to know from the outset that many mindfulness teacher-training programmes require a commitment to personal practice and that some have significant prerequisites. On page 108 we outline possible pathways if you want to go on to teach mindfulness to students.

Wanting to teach this stuff (or in fact, any social, emotional or ethical skill) to kids because we think it will be 'good for them' doesn't really work - or even make sense - unless we, too, are involved in developing the same desirable capacities in ourselves. We wouldn't start teaching people how to drive a car - even if we could work out how to do so from a course or a book - unless we could already drive ourselves. The normal nature of school professional development is to go and learn something and then be ready to teach our colleagues. But mindfulness training is not your average professional development. First, you can't suddenly become a teacher of mindfulness. It takes time. Most schools and many educators are primed to feel that any investment of time in professional development must lead to some immediately visible dividend in the classroom. But for mindfulness to take root and thrive within an educational organisation, it needs careful tending and slow organic development. Many aspects of mindfulness training appear very simple, but it's also easy to teach them in a way that misses the point or that turns kids off. It is essential therefore that we practice it in some depth for ourselves first, so that we have a full understanding of the various aspects of mindfulness and are then able to lead and speak from personal experience, not just theory.

STOP AND BREATHE

In 2008 I started to try out teaching simple meditation exercises to students at my middle school at the International School of Prague, where I was Principal.

Later I began looking around for a programme I could use and came across the .b – or *Stop & Be* – course for teenagers. This programme from the Mindfulness in Schools Project (MiSP) was just then getting started in the UK, developed by three educators: Richard Burnett, Chris Cullen and Chris O'Neil. It was a natural fit for my classes – skilfully designed for teenage students by combining a variety of engaging practices with entertaining slides and videos – and it enabled the young people I was teaching to access the learning in a way that went far beyond my own initial efforts.

Recently in the UK, the Wellcome Trust has funded a major research programme co-led by the University of Oxford, University College London, the Medical Research Council Cognition and Brain Sciences Unit at Cambridge University, with support from the University of Exeter and a number of international collaborators. The programme involves several research themes, and includes studies examining the short-term effects of mindfulness training on adolescent psychological functioning; the implementation of mindfulness in schools (including the relative effectiveness of different forms of mindfulness training); and a large-scale, longitudinal, randomised control research trial. The trial, which started in 2015, aims to recruit 76 schools (304 teachers and 5,700 pupils) from across the UK. In half the schools participating teachers and pupils will be trained in mindfulness to establish the impact of the training on students' emotional health and wellbeing. This £6.5m MYRIAD (Mindfulness and Resilience in Adolescence) project will track students for approximately two years after completing their training. The course selected as the vehicle for this research is the '.b' programme.

From time to time I will draw on the Mindfulness in Schools Project's programmes for teenagers and for primary students to give readers a feel for how mindfulness can be introduced in school settings. These youth courses are based on the MBCT and MBSR programmes described in Chapter 2, and in particular they draw on the MBCT work of Mark Williams from Oxford University's Oxford Mindfulness Centre. I sometimes work as a teacher trainer for the MiSP programmes and I am using these courses as examples of mindful awareness training in schools because, as a teacher, they are the ones I know best, and because I have found they work well for students. On page 108 there is a list of other programmes that you might also want to consider if you are planning to introduce mindfulness training to your school.

DIFFERENT KETTLES OF FISH – TRAINING ADULTS AND TRAINING STUDENTS

Adults may come to mindfulness because they are suffering mentally or physically or they may have run out of other options or, for some, because they have simply chosen to explore this wonderful, life-giving experience. But with students, especially middle- and high-school students, it's not often the case that they are choosing to take a course in mindfulness. The courses that we teach in schools are not clinical or therapeutic programmes, they are designed as introductions to mindfulness. These experiential classes provide a degree of training and a chance to develop some inner awareness and new skills that can be applied in a variety of ways, but overall the intention is for young people to get a feel for what mindful awareness is about, what it can do for them and especially to know that it's there and available so that, later on in life, if they face difficult experiences they know there are ways to get help. An important learning point for teenagers is that you can become an active agent in your own mental emotional and physical wellbeing.

MINDFUL AWARENESS TRAINING IN SCHOOLS

Mindful awareness training can offer students – and educators – an introduction that will:

- help them understand, intellectually and experientially, some key aspects of how their minds, bodies and emotions work

- develop some key capacities of self-awareness and of sustaining attention

- empower them to be able to respond more wisely in some challenging situations.

We will illustrate how this can be achieved with some examples of mindfulness programmes for primary and secondary students. Please note that the examples in this chapter are simply to give you a taste of what this looks like, not to equip you to deliver the exercises described.

In an introductory MiSP session a central message about mindfulness is given to students by referring to a lovely segment of the *Kung Fu Panda* movie (Dreamworks Animation and Paramount Pictures, 2008) where Po, the panda, is interrupted in the midst of beating himself up after a bad day by the wise old turtle, Oogway:

'You are too concerned with what was, and what will be.

There is a saying you know,

'Yesterday is History,

Tomorrow is a Mystery,

But Today is a Gift;

That is why it is called The Present.'

After introducing students to this core theme, teachers will usually explain what mindfulness is, look at some of the science behind it, and at how it can be helpful for us in school and in our lives. Theory can only get you so far though, so with mindfulness introductions the key is that students (and teachers) *experience* it firsthand.

PAY ATTENTION!

'Mindfulness is ... the awareness that arises when we pay attention, on purpose ...'

The first full session of the course moves straight into understanding how we can train our minds to be able to sustain a deeper form of attention. Given the plethora of distractions bombarding us these days and the distractibility of our modern minds, it is highly important for young people to be trained in building attention skills. Stanford researcher Philippe Goldin once said 'Parents and teachers tell kids 100 times a day to pay attention. But we never teach them how' (Brown, 2007).

This first lesson teaches children to *'play* attention' as opposed to feeling forced to *pay* attention. With a light touch students are guided into an experience of moving their attention around the body. You can see (and experience) a TEDx Talk of Richard Burnett from MiSP introducing mindfulness in education at www.youtube.com/watch?v=6mlk6xD_xAQ.

If you can, watch it in a quiet space so you can try out the brief exercises he leads in the first 10 minutes of the session. Such exercises are often used in the introductory sessions with students and are always followed by an 'inquiry' – a chance for students to reflect in pairs on their experience and then to take a few examples from the whole class. This is a crucial point because it is here that we have a chance to discover that it is totally normal to have a mind that wanders.

Because of this natural tendency of our minds to wander, Jack Kornfield, author of *A Path with Heart* (1993), compared training the mind to training a puppy. The MiSP programmes for children build on this analogy in their attention training exercises, showing how the qualities we need to cultivate on a journey into mindful awareness can be quite similar to those needed to train a puppy; that is, *firmness, patience and kindness.*

By the end of this initial 40–60 minute class we are usually able to have established experientially three key concepts:

1. We can choose where to put our attention.

2. When we try to keep our attention in one place it doesn't easily stay there (the mind wanders).

3. We can learn strategies to improve our capacity to attend.

Attention is also important because what we attend to gets strengthened. If you are a taxi driver, the part of your brain that deals with navigation, the posterior hippocampus, grows larger than average (Maguire et al., 2006); and if you are a violinist, the areas of the brain that deal with finger coordination grow denser connections (Elbert et al., 1995).

William James, one of the key figures in the development of psychology as a modern science, underlined the importance of attention:

The faculty of voluntarily bringing back a wandering attention over and over again is the very root of judgement, character and will. An education which should improve this faculty would be the education par excellence.

But it is easier to define this ideal than to give practical instructions for bringing it about. (James, 1890)

Thanks to the developments outlined in Chapter 2, well-designed, evidence-based programmes from organisations such as the *Mindfulness in Schools Project* (UK) and *Mindful Schools* (USA) are now doing exactly what James described, in a way that wasn't conceivable in the West at the end of the 19th century.

THE ATTENTION SPAN OF A GOLDFISH

In 2013–14, Microsoft surveyed 2,000 Canadians and carried out brain mapping with over 100 of them to explore the issue of attention in relation to screen use (Microsoft, 2015). The results showed that our average attention span is declining – from 12 seconds in 2000 to 8 seconds in 2013. (Embarrassingly, Microsoft say this is less than the 9-second attention span of a goldfish, so all those jokes about the attention spans of a goldfish will have to stop!) The report concluded that 'Overall, digital lifestyles have a negative impact on prolonged focus' and listed the top factors that impact attention as:

- Media consumption
- Social media usage
- Technology adoption rate
- Multi-screening behaviour

Studies such as this indicate that our screen-based lifestyle may be eroding some aspects of our capacity to sustain focus. We may not simply be losing our overall ability to pay attention, it may be that we are now using it in different ways. Out of necessity in the digital age, we are increasing our tendency to multitask, or actually to be able to cope with multiple sources of information, juggling them and moving between them. The brain seems to be plastic enough to enable this to happen, but it comes at a cost: sustained focus. This same plasticity, however, may also allow us to retrain the brain – to increase our attention span – if we devote the time and energy to doing so.

And we should want to right now because, wonderful as it is to be able to surf the net and discover all sorts of things we would never have known about without spending years in a public library, we also need to develop and preserve the ability to sustain attention. In Chapter 6 we explore how our ability to truly attend, to listen deeply, and to experience being heard, are fundamental to our human connectivity.

FOCUSING

In *Focus* (2013) psychologist Daniel Goleman illustrates how worry and other distracting emotions can intrude on a student's capacity to fully attend to their work. He expresses concern about the impact on children of our modern technological environment through the reduction of direct personal interaction and he argues that increased interaction with digital screens can pose a threat to the neuronal development of our social and emotional circuitry, as well as the reduction in sustained engagement noted above. Goleman claims that this is already beginning to show up in schools, where, for example, some middle school students find sustained reading too taxing for them. All this, he says, points to the need to learn the skills of self-awareness that enable us to notice when we might be losing focus and then to refocus. He advocates strongly for 'programs, like mindfulness, that boost the brain's executive control' (Goleman, 2013: 205).

Goleman also underlines the importance of training attention skills to strengthen self-control – a key factor in life satisfaction. He describes a major study in New Zealand that tracked all babies born in a 12-month period in the town of Dunedin (over 1,000 children) for over 20 years and found that *self-control* was as good a predictor of success in life as *class, IQ* or *family*. ('Success' was defined here as health, wealth and good behaviour.) (Moffitt et al., 2011). Goleman asks, because of the significance of learning self-control, 'Wouldn't it make sense to teach these skills to every child?' (2013: 206).

As William James pointed out over a century ago, the ability to sustain attention is the key to deep learning. Having the self-awareness and the discipline to recognise what we don't know or what we can't do so well and then redirecting our attention to go over those areas again until we do, is a fundamental skill in education. Training in mindful awareness can be a highly effective means of developing this capacity (Sanger and Dorjee, 2016) and has the potential also of promoting positive mental health and helping lay the foundations for a life well-lived.

STANLEY GROVE PRIMARY SCHOOL, MANCHESTER, UK

Stanley Grove primary school serves the multi-cultural community of Longsight, an inner-city disadvantaged area in Manchester. There is a vibrant local community where most people have emigrated from Eastern Europe, North Africa and South Asia. Over 90 per cent of the students at the school are Muslim, and they all get the chance to learn mindfulness (8-week courses are currently taught to all children aged 8-10 years).

> We have introduced mindfulness training because some studies have shown that the onset of mental health problems is now peaking at age 11 and we want to help give children a better understanding of how their minds work and to give them strategies to cope with the difficulties that they'll face as adolescents. With all the technology these days, children spend a lot of their time in thinking mode or in front of screens, and mindfulness gives them a chance to step away from that and spend a bit of time in their bodies more than in their heads.

> We use the 'Paws b' programme [a course for 7-11-year-olds] from the Mindfulness in Schools Project which has loads of analogies and metaphors so we'll use the fact that our attention is like a torch light and that you can focus it in different ways. We look at a snow globe and talk about the fact that our mind can get really busy, just like when you shake up a snow globe and all the little flakes flutter around. We use that to help them understand

that there are times when our minds are just full of things and sometimes you can't really think clearly or see clearly and actually by doing a short practice you can help bring your focus back down into your body, into your sensing mode more than your thinking mode and allow that dust to clear.

Our children say that they use it to calm themselves down, they use it when they are dealing with difficulty, so they'll talk about squabbles and falling out at home, they talk about using it before tests. One girl talked about getting over her fear of swimming lessons by using mindfulness practices. The practice helps them sense things in the body a bit more so we'll get them to notice, just by being still, things like, 'Oh I'm clenching my jaw'; or you might know that when you are stressed your shoulders might rise up. For different people there are different triggers, so just by noticing those in yourself it allows you then to have a choice - rather than reacting impulsively you get to choose to perhaps respond in a different way.

We've had research studies done in our school and found that children's attention and concentration improves. But there's also those anecdotal things that teachers talk about - their children having much better focus in lessons, better behaviours for learning, just being able to leave all the playground squabbles at the door and being more ready to learn when they are in class.

It doesn't work for everyone of course, but sometimes you just need to get it at a time when it's right for you. One 8-year-old pupil I taught in year 4 said 'Don't get it Miss, don't like it, it's boring.' Then I taught the same curriculum again in year 5. Half way through the year something clicked for her and now she speaks passionately about how she uses the practice to control her nerves before tests and performing.

Amy Footman, Head of Stanley Grove

HEARTFULNESS - MORE THAN JUST 'BARE ATTENTION'

'Mindfulness is, paying attention ... on purpose, *with curiosity and kindness* ...'

So, is mindfulness simply 'bare attention training'?

Attention training is a key component of mindfulness but it's not the whole deal. You could, for example, use attention training to improve your ability to stealthily pick off human targets through a sniper's rifle telescope, but this would not qualify as mindfulness. The *quality* of attention that we bring to any moment is fundamental. 'Mindfulness' itself is the word chosen by Christian academics seeking to translate the Pali word *sati*. *Sati* is used by Buddhists to describe a purposeful remembering to be present that is as much 'heartful' as it is 'mindful'.

Buddhist monks in the Himalayas who were subjects for a Harvard University research team in the 1970s literally fell on the floor laughing when the researchers wired up their heads for the experiment. They couldn't believe Westerners thought the mind was in the head:

> When we put an electrode cap on Francisco Varela's head to measure EEG waves all the monks burst out laughing as though we'd told them the most hilarious joke. They were amused that we were using a device placed on the scalp to measure the mind when, to them, it was obvious that the mind is not in the head, but located at one's heart. (Saron, 2013)

'Heartfulness' – learning to turn towards our experiences and to other people in an open, kind, non-judgmental way – is at the core of mindful awareness training.

The Chinese character for 'mindfulness' (see Figure 5.1) is actually a pictogram portraying the 'present moment' sheltering the symbol for 'heart' (sometimes translated as 'heartmind').

Figure 5.1 The Chinese character for 'mindfulness'

Humans are naturally curious and creative, and our social evolution depends upon these capacities. Mindful attention has a certain natural quality of curiosity and kindness that brings a warmth to our experience, and to our connection with self and with others. This sense of a heartful presence can be developed through mindfulness training – sometimes arising spontaneously, sometimes cultivated consciously to deepen our sense of connection. There is a degree of empathy that can occur naturally when we understand more about our own minds and emotions and when we come to understand that others are often struggling with similar issues and experiences. Whilst the popular impression might be that mindful awareness can be just a quick attention fix, in reality empathy and compassion are profound and essential elements of the practice of mindfulness. Stephen Covey wrote that 'Between stimulus and response, there is a space. In that space is our power to choose our response. In our response lies our growth and our freedom' (Pattakos, 2004). Covey was using this passage (that he had read in a now forgotten source) to try to describe one of Viktor Frankl's hard-won psychological insights about the fact that inner freedom can sometimes be discovered in the most inhospitable conditions. Frankl observed how some of his fellow prisoners in concentration camps in Nazi Germany were able to draw on deep sources of empathy and compassion even when they were in the midst of severe suffering. Some neuroscientists are these days investigating precisely what it is about mindfulness training that might help buy us the time between stimulus and response to make wiser choices about our actions and interactions. The author of one such study, Micah Allen, says,

> As we begin to realize that many societal and health problems cannot be solved through medication or attention-training alone, it becomes clear that techniques to increase emotional function and well-being are crucial for future development ...
>
> I suspect we need to begin including affective processes in our understanding of optimal learning. (Allen, 2012)

For Professor Richie Davidson, Head of the Laboratory for Affective Neuroscience at the University of Wisconsin, wellbeing is a skill:

> Well-being is fundamentally no different than learning to play the cello. If one practices the skills of well-being, one will get better at it. (Davidson, 2016)

Davidson's conclusion is based on laboratory studies carried out with volunteers and with long-term meditators. Empathy and compassion are innate capacities that we all share, though of course they may come more easily to some than others. The key point in the context of this book is that they can all be consciously developed. They are all interpersonal skills that can be trained and mindful awareness training is a foundational approach that can support the development of these emotional intelligences in schools.

Professor Davidson, speaking to the CASEL Forum in New York in 2007, said,

> Social and emotional learning is an empirically verified strategy to improve skills of emotional regulation and social adaptation. Qualities such as calmness, cooperation and kindness are all best regarded as skills that can be trained. Training like Social Emotional Learning can shape the brain – and literally change gene expression.
>
> (The full video is available at www.edutopia.org/richard-davidson-sel-brain-video)

Even if compassion itself isn't listed as a subject within a mindfulness programme, by the very nature of the course we would expect empathy and compassion to be modelled by the teacher and to find expression in the learning environment and in the learning relationships that are formed. It has been my experience that even without an explicit focus on the cultivation of compassion and empathy, mindful awareness training in schools can help promote these qualities. Mindfulness is never just about 'bare attention'; by fostering a kindly, focused awareness and by building our capacity to turn toward difficulties with equanimity we are laying the foundation for an empathetic and compassionate connectedness.

Some courses have been developed for training these skills to students and teachers, again based on traditional approaches combined with research in neuroscience.

One example is the Kindness Curriculum from the Centre for Investigating Healthy Minds, University of Wisconsin-Madison (see Pinger and Flook, 2016). See also the work of Dr Kristin Neff (http://self-compassion.org/).

UNDERSTANDING OUR MIND, BODY AND EMOTIONS

We are born with a mind-body system that has evolved over millennia to equip us as best it can with the means to survive. It's an amazing, incredible piece of engineering - but it's not a perfect package and our emotions and thoughts don't always function the way we would like them to. However evolved we may think we are, our impulses and reactions can still take us by surprise and we are all capable at times of an inappropriate response, especially when unwell or under pressure. Much of our work as educators in this field revolves around the question:

> 'Can we help prepare young people to cope more effectively with life's ups and downs, and with our sometimes clumsy reactions to the inevitable difficulties and challenges that come our way?'

Some classes in youth mindfulness programmes are directly aimed at improving our understanding of how our minds, bodies and emotions work together - and how they can sometimes trip us up. An example of a practical application of cultivating self-awareness used with teenagers in the MiSP '.b' programme is to ask them what might be their response if, having recently met someone they really liked and swapped phone numbers with them, they wait hopefully for a response to a sent text but no response arrives.

This is fertile ground for teenagers, and some groups will come up with a rich range of reactions. Some are positive:

> 'They might have dropped the phone down the toilet or run out of battery.'

But most commonly they tend to be quite negative (and ultimately self-deprecating):

> 'Maybe I said something stupid?'

> 'Maybe they never really liked me and just wanted to get away?'

> 'Why do I always get things wrong?'

> 'Why doesn't anyone really like me ...?'

NEGATIVITY BIAS

Our organism has a natural propensity to err on the side of caution when facing a threatening situation in order to protect us. This sometimes creates what's

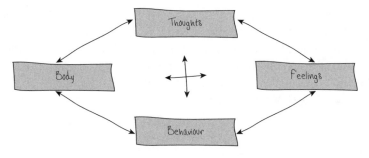

Figure 5.2 Cognitive behaviour model

often referred to as an inbuilt 'negativity bias'. Many of the activities in mindful awareness courses help children understand this inner bias more explicitly. We use the cognitive behaviour model (see Figure 5.2) to help students understand the interconnectedness of feelings, thoughts, sensations and actions/impulses. In this way, we can learn to start to tease apart these elements that might lie intertwined beneath a mood or might trigger a reaction.

We introduce the idea that while some of our thoughts and stories may be true, some may not be. This can sometimes lead to quite profound insights for teenagers as they begin to understand our instinctive tendency to create stories around experiences. A number of teenagers I have worked with on mindful aware-ness courses have told me that gaining this understanding – that 'thoughts are not facts' – has been a highly significant learning experience for them.

'I've already used that bit about Thoughts Aren't Facts because two weeks ago me and my friends got in a big fight. One thought this way, and then the others were against him so when my teacher said that 'thoughts aren't facts' I started to look at what his point of view is and then we understood that the problem wasn't actually between us, it was between someone else trying to separate us.'

12-year-old student

There is a beautiful Tibetan simile that describes how thoughts and feelings come and go like 'writing on water' – a helpful illustration of the insubstantial quality of thinking. But these silent wisps of wind on water don't always seem so vacuous to us, they often feel quite concrete and they can sometimes have considerable power over us, especially when unexamined. It's not just our students who struggle with this – as I write this paragraph, for example, I am aware that the date I had expected to hear back from a publisher is now passed. At first this won't be a prob-lem, but as time goes by, I might begin to wonder if my proposal was really good enough, and on a bad day I might even wonder if anybody is really interested. The negativity bias, combined with our incessant inner narrative, can cause all of us problems at times. Because many of us live with strong inner critics, we sometimes need to consciously notice the positive things, relationships and experiences in our lives, to take the time to appreciate and be grateful for what we do have. Mindful awareness courses, especially when combined with social-emotional training or positive psychology, can help some young people learn the value of appreciation and gratitude on an experiential level.

PATTERN COMPLETION

We tend to assume that our visual experience of a sequence of moments is similar to a video camera that scans around a room, taking in everything it sees. But neuroscience has discovered that our visual mechanism actually works more like an old-fashioned film reel, with its moving compilation of single frames. Our perceived experience is a collage of blurry images that our brain assembles, synthesising visual data with auditory and other sensory information being received at that moment, and turning it into an apparently natural flow that becomes our view of reality (Lau and Rosenthal, 2011).

It's this deep-seated ability to complete patterns, to take small chunks of information and weave them into a coherent whole, that lies at the heart of our human predisposition to storytelling. Even with limited data we jump to conclusions and form assumptions. If there are a few dots on a page, we might see lines and patterns and predict trajectories, real or imagined.

Where, for instance, might your mind go if the teacher in the following scenario was you?

It's Friday afternoon and you are doing some last minute photocopying before heading home. The Head passes by, sees you, hesitates and then says, 'Oh, I need to have a word with you. Can you pop in to see me on Monday morning?'

You respond with a quick 'Yes, sure' and before you know it she's gone, leaving you wondering.

Driving home, and periodically over the weekend, you mull over what it can be about. All the challenging situations and exchanges you had with students, colleagues or parents over the past few weeks come to mind. Who has been complaining about you? Was it that time you over-reacted when the Year 9 girls were messing around in class? Or were you too honest with Mr and Mrs Duckworth about their son's learning difficulties last week?

Round and round you go until Monday morning and before school you are at the Head's door.

'Good morning,' she says, 'How are you? What can I do for you?'

'You asked me to pass by?'

'I did? Oh yes, Friday afternoon, right, sorry, I had a lot going on then. No, I just wanted to talk to you about your Year 10 History project.'

'I see.'

'Yes, at the open parent session last week there were a number of parents talking about how much their children had enjoyed the practical challenges you set the students.'

'They did?'

'That's right. I was wondering if you might do some in-house training with the Year 8 team – they need to move in that direction too. I do think you're really doing some great work this year.'

NATURAL–BORN STORYTELLERS

This inner narrative mode, that can sometimes be quite self-critical, is so constant and ingrained that most of the time we don't even notice it. Mindfulness can help us become more aware of the subtle layers of thought and sensation that often drive our everyday behaviour. It's this awareness that can give us the freedom to choose an appropriate response rather than be driven by an inappropriate reaction.

The understanding that we can develop our ability *to notice the stories we tell about ourselves and about others* can also be applied on a cultural or political level. To question, for example, popular stories and misconceptions about refugees, immigrants or climate change that might stand in the way of wise action. If we become more aware of the stories and subliminal messages that our group, party, nation, religion or culture feed us, then we might begin to examine them more carefully and to question if they are telling us a truth, exposing a fear or a prejudice, or perhaps masking a need to maintain superiority.

ACCOMMODATING COMPETING NARRATIVES

Loosening the constraints of cultural conditioning can be achieved in various ways: travel is one way that helped me to do this, and developing awareness through deep dialogue with others, or through meditation, are others. I love the phrase used by Israeli writer Yossi Halevi when he asks if it is possible, as an Israeli or a Palestinian, to learn to 'accommodate competing narratives' (2002). To know, for example, that I have a story about your culture, and yet still be able to hear *your* story about *your* culture. This is such an important area, both in conflict resolution and in terms of forging greater understanding between people, genders, races and cultures. In learning how best to 'share the planet', this is a key skill that we must help develop in our young people.

While writing this book I was informed by a colleague in the USA, Rona Wilensky, about recent work looking at the connection between mindfulness and social justice in issues related to race, ethnicity, gender and age. These are key areas these days for all of us to explore and support. Rona told me of a network of professionals currently exploring the interdependence of these two movements – especially in the area of bias.

One person active in this emerging field is Rhonda Magee, Professor of Law at the University of San Francisco and a Visiting Scholar at the Berkeley Center for the Study of Law and Society. Contributing to a series of articles on mindfulness and the criminal justice system published by The Greater Good Centre at Berkeley Magee says,

> As most of us know from simple, everyday experience, none of us is actually blind to race or color. In fact, research confirms common disconnects between explicit and implicit cognition around race and color. Even if we try to adopt a colorblind view in the world, it doesn't work because our brains don't actually work that way
> (Magee, 2015)

Magee has adapted contemplative practices to help people cultivate greater awareness of bias and says that these exercises can, 'Pave the way to new experiences that help us loosen our attachments to narratives and other forms of suffering that give rise to biases along the way' (Magee, 2015). One research study that supports Magee's work focused on the impact of mindfulness on implicit age and racial bias and found that, 'Mindfulness meditation caused a decrease...in implicit race and age bias...due to weaker automatically activated associations on the Implicit Attitude Test' (Lueke and Gibson, 2014). This study indicated that participants who took the mindfulness training relied less on previously established associations and suggested that even a 10-minute mindfulness practice can begin to reduce race and age bias.

Mindful awareness can, then, help stop us from getting 'hooked' by our stories and help us see that thoughts can be fallible. Understanding how our minds and emotions work can help us to connect more authentically in relationship, and we can come to understand that, whilst negative stories might isolate us, a more open awareness brings us closer together.

STANLEY CHAN, EDUCATIONAL PSYCHOLOGIST WITH CHILDREN WITH SPECIAL NEEDS, HONG KONG

We did a pilot trial for children with ADHD (8–12-year-olds). We worked with the children and with the parents, teaching them mindfulness. Parents reported that children's behaviour improved. They also said they felt higher empathy and acceptance toward their children and reported that their emotional control was better. They are less likely to get angry and they can stay calmer in their daily interactions with the children. In addition, they felt their self-care had been enhanced – that they feel it is important to take care of themselves. The preliminary results indicate the programme may be effective in reducing the stress of the parents, reducing depressive symptoms and especially reducing the stress from parent–child dysfunctional interactions.

We use the metaphor of ferry safety: 'Parents need to learn to help themselves before helping their children.'

I have also tried teaching mindfulness to students with autism. It was quite good. The kids found it interesting and it helped them to enhance their awareness of their emotions and helped them to be more calm and to deal with stress. Sometimes autistic students can have tunnel vision and maybe this can help them expand it. One of the parents told me that in the past his son would complain about this and that in the school but after the programme he was taking things more easily.

In the last school year there were quite a number of suicide cases in HK. It is very stressful in HK in students' studies, so I think this is very important.

(Research Autism (2016) and de Bruin et al. (2015) are excellent sources for finding out more about research into mindfulness and autism).

(Personal communication, February 2016)

EVIDENCE FOR THE BENEFITS OF MINDFULNESS FOR CHILDREN AND YOUNG PEOPLE

The research that has been carried out with children so far has largely yielded positive results. However, it is important to recognise that, in research terms, this is still very much an 'emergent' area. What research has been done with children has, until recently, been mainly small scale, and larger-scale, long-term studies such as the MYRIAD trial are only just beginning.

(Continued)

(Continued)

Extrapolating, though, from the positive research on mindfulness with adults, it seems likely that introducing young people to mindfulness could have important benefits in terms of promoting positive mental health and raising awareness. In general we wouldn't expect to see the same depth of impact with school populations as with adults because training for children is usually introductory; it is not clinical, it is often involuntary, and it normally entails far fewer hours of practice.

In October 2015 a report was published in the UK by the Mindfulness All-Party Parliamentary Group. This committee of MPs and peers from the main political parties met with experts over a 12-month period to consider the potential of mindfulness in mental health, justice, the workplace and education. Their findings were compiled in the report *Mindful Nation UK* (MAPPG, 2015).

After examining a wide range of evidence, the group made a strong recommendation to the UK government to invest in research and workplace practice to further mindful awareness training in schools. Their summary of the evidence on mindfulness is a useful starting point if you are interested in finding out more about the research:

> There is promising evidence that mindfulness training has been shown to enhance executive control in children and adolescents in line with adult evidence. Recent meta-analyses of Mindfulness Based Interventions for children and adolescents suggested improvements in stress, anxiety, depression, emotional behavioural regulation, with larger effects reported in clinical than non-clinical populations. ... What is of particular interest is that those with the lowest levels of executive control and emotional stability are likely to benefit most from mindfulness training. (MAPPG, 2015)

The report goes on to emphasise how reducing stress and improving self-regulation has a positive impact on academic performance and points out the potential for combining mindfulness with social-emotional learning (our main focus in Chapter 6). The politicians draw attention to the potential, from the research, for mindfulness training to help with behavioural difficulties and with attention deficit disorders – helping children deal with 'impulsiveness, aggression and oppositional behaviour'.

Below is a small sample of other studies on mindfulness with children across the age ranges:

- A 2015 study with 7–9-year-olds taking an 8-week mindfulness course showed a reduction in negative affect (mood) and improvement in self-management in relation to organisation of schoolwork (Vickery and Dorjee, 2016).

- Hennelly (2010) studied the impact of the '.b' mindfulness course on 11–17-year-olds and found there were significant differences between the participant and control groups in terms of mindfulness, resilience and well-being. Students, teachers and parents reported subjective improvements in students' academic motivation, confidence, competence and effectiveness.

- A feasibility study for the MYRIAD trial was carried out in 2013 by Oxford and Exeter Universities (Kuyken et al., 2013) and found that students completing an 8-week youth mindfulness course experienced greater wellbeing and saw significant reductions in depression and stress.

- Research with students has not often involved brain scans, but a 2016 study (Sanger and Dorjee) with 16–18-year-olds used EEGs to measure attention performance on computerised distraction tests. The results clearly correlated self-reported levels of distractibility with EEG evidence of improvement on focusing tasks, suggesting 'that adolescents trained in mindfulness-based practices were able to discriminately inhibit responses to task-irrelevant stimuli'. In other words, they could focus better after the training and, importantly, given the current exposure to digital overload, were able to 'more efficiently inhibit irrelevant stimuli'. The students also displayed reduced hypercritical self-beliefs compared with the control group.

- A robust, large-scale randomised clinical trial (Biegel et al., 2009) with both primary and secondary aged students followed children aged 4–18 years who had a range of mental health diagnoses. After taking a modified MBSR programme the students reported significantly reduced symptoms of anxiety and depression, as well as increased self-esteem and sleep quality, compared with control groups.

For a large-scale, detailed review of mindfulness-based interventions in school settings in USA, see the paper by Felver et al. (2015). For a review of 15 studies from around the world looking at the effectiveness of mindfulness in improving mental health symptoms of children and adolescents, see Kallapiran et al. (2015).

Another helpful starting point when looking at the evidence on mindfulness for children and young people is a paper written in 2013 by Katherine Weare, Emeritus Professor at the University of Exeter and Southampton. Weare outlines a range of studies showing positive results from using mindfulness with children and adolescents, including studies on:

- executive function for primary school children

- anxiety for primary school children

- self-regulation for primary school children from disadvantaged backgrounds

- 9–13-year-olds with academic difficulties

- 10–13-year-olds with behaviour problems and depression

- learning difficulties with secondary school students.

(Continued)

(Continued)

'Conclusions have to be tentative at this stage. However, the results of a wide range of studies in different contexts offer a set of promising results that suggest that mindfulness is well worth doing.

It would appear that when children and young people learn to be more 'present' and less anxious they can pay attention better and improve the quality of their performance, in the classroom, on the sports field and in the performing arts for example. They often become more focused, more able to approach situations from a fresh perspective, use existing knowledge more effectively, and pay attention.

Young people generally enjoy and appreciate the interventions, and the processes and the effects of mindfulness on the young are very similar to the positive changes observable in adults which gives cause for optimism that the same psychological and physiological processes are at work.' (Weare, 2013).

These conclusions are coming from a range of research targeting specific groups with specific interventions. It is important to not over-claim results from research studies and assume they prove something that will be of benefit in any context. We may not, for example, expect an introductory, compulsory class in a secondary school to have long-lasting, measurable impacts for large numbers of students. However, for many individuals it can be highly significant, and for all students it could be a meaningful addition to the skills-based learning that our schools offer young people. I know from my work with children and teachers that many do feel the courses have been very beneficial to them, and if we can evolve a spiralling curriculum of integrated social-emotional mindfulness-based activities in schools, then we are likely to find a deepening of the positive effects that current research is indicating. Even if students don't use the skills they learn right away, you never know in the long run when it may prove to be of benefit – if only because young people will know that help and training for mental health is available if they need it.

A helpful collection of fact sheets on research on mindfulness in education is available from the Canadian website *Discover Mindfulness* (available at http://discovermindfulness.ca/tool-kit/).

PUPIL HEALTH REFERRAL UNIT TEACHER, UK

This unit works with students who are not attending school or had a very limited timetable. They are out of school for many different reasons, health problems (mostly mental health issues) as well as bullying and non-attendance. Some are undergoing other therapies like CBT with Child and Adolescent Mental Health Services. All students were taught mindfulness classes in PSHE on the normal school timetable.

Over time we have seen big changes. 75 per cent were hitting the targets for high anxiety on the *Strengths and Difficulties Questionnaire* which then went down to 35 per cent four years later. I can't say that was all to do with mindfulness because we have done all sorts of things in a nurturing environment. But what I noticed with the mindfulness was the ability for students to have some skills for themselves, so they weren't relying on other people to calm them down or recognise things, for example if they were getting anxious or having difficulties in relationships. We have built a kind of ethos in the school that makes it okay to 'feel your feet on the floor' or 'take a breath'. Before it was all about talking it through with someone, so there has been a definite shift in the children using mindfulness in an active and acceptable way.

Some of our pupils identified themselves very much with their illnesses. Some used their symptoms as a reason for not participating in activities and they would say, 'I'm too tired, I'm depressed' but we gave them some skills to have some distance, which enabled them to notice and recognise their symptoms and make more informed choices. They could recognise that the symptoms were just the symptoms and not them as a person.

One boy came to me one day in the corridor and said, 'Miss, I feel like I'm going to get a panic attack, is it okay to do a sitting practice?'

And a young girl who had a diagnosis of ADHD and was one of the most restless pupils said, after a bodyscan, 'I don't think I've ever been that still and calm ever'. It just seemed to be able to help her manage her symptoms of restlessness.

Of course we have had many challenges. There was a fair bit of cynicism when we first started. There were many misconceptions about what we were doing. And then we had difficulty with continuity and attendance and making sure that pupils who started it followed through. Some kids liked it, some said 'It's not for me' or 'We'll get a good sleep here'. I try to be very careful how I deal with those students and how I model it. Classroom management is very important - to allow opportunities for all to engage with it at their own level.

When I actually saw the benefits in our unit I thought, all pupils need the opportunity to learn this approach. It was helping our students cope with their often chaotic lives. It's really important and something that can potentially help them in their future lives.

Anonymous Personal communication, July 2016

HOW DO STUDENTS SAY THEY USE MINDFUL AWARENESS?

In terms of how children actually use this developing understanding of themselves, there is no prescribed list of learning outcomes. It's rather, as the MiSP puts it, an exploration of 'possibilities'. Children taking introductory courses in mindfulness don't necessarily do much home practice but the majority seem to apply some mindfulness exercises in daily life. Some students speak enthusiastically about how the training has helped them focus more in class, or cope with anxiety in exams, or in musical or dramatic performances. Some say they apply the breathing and grounding techniques in sports to help them focus and calm themselves (many students I know have used it a lot in basketball, for example just before a free throw). Some have used it to help contain or channel anger or nervousness. Some talk about how it has helped them relate better to family or friends, quite often reporting using a mindful moment, or taking a breath to help manage themselves in an argument with parents or with an annoying sibling.

Here are a few examples of how children of various ages, taught by myself and by colleagues, say they have used some of the strategies they learned from mindful awareness courses:

Even though I only had nine lessons they were really helpful to me because it gave me a time to kind of sit back for an hour and reflect on the things that were going on in my courses and do an activity that wasn't necessarily academically inclined. It was something a little bit different and in that regard I think it was a really positive experience. The practice I remember most is 7/11 breathing and I've actually used it a couple of times this year. I gave a speech and I was quite nervous before my speech and I did 7/11 breathing and it calmed me down quite a bit. I've also been trying to do things when I go to bed with kind of focusing my energy. I know some people who were hesitant to be a part of it really enjoyed it in the end and I think what you get out of it is especially useful for the IB students and the IB curriculum and I definitely think it should be compulsory.

17-year-old boy

I have learned to recognise if I am worrying and recognise if things are difficult just to let it be difficult and just do it - not over thinking about 'Oh no it's difficult I'm going to fail and I'm not going to be any good' and jump to conclusions. Just let it be and acknowledge its difficultness. I mean I do have my moments when I'm all totally freaking out and thinking about failing college and everything but I really think it helps and I totally recommend it to everyone.

18-year-old girl

I don't know how to explain it but the class was really exciting and fun to be in and really calm and everything. Tomorrow on stage I'll be acting and I think it would really help me to breathe because usually I get really stressed when I'm performing in front of a lot of people. I memorise lines and everything and I'm scared I'll forget them but whenever I breathe it helps me a lot.

12-year-old girl

Mindfulness is good because it can help you like, calm down and for like people who are stressed with exams and stuff it's like a moment of peace and silence so you can concentrate on your brain so when it comes to the test you don't get distracted by somebody talking. I do it maybe before sleeping sometimes like once a week it helps like communicate with your insides. When you think about what could be inside there's like blood cells and everything inside and you just put your attention to everything inside.

10-year-old boy

I'd say if you are stressed and you are not feeling like yourself for a day or so you can try out mindfulness and it affects you because it lets you communicate with your inner body. I would say it's for all people – anybody can do it. If you are not feeling that calm and you did a test and you are waiting for your results and you want to get high marks and then I would say that you could do a bit of mindfulness. So then the thoughts are going away and on the day when it comes you won't be that stressed out even if you get low marks.

10-year-old girl

EMMA NAISBETT PRIMARY SCHOOL TEACHER ENGLISH MARTYRS SCHOOL (3-11 YEARS) SOUTHPORT, LIVERPOOL, UK

For me the biggest impact on the children is in their self-regulation of emotions and their resilience. The kind of shared awareness that actually thoughts are not necessarily true and that they have a choice in how they can respond to thoughts that they may have. I think this has had a huge impact on self-confidence, self-esteem and self-belief. When perhaps children are faced with something tricky or that they feel nervous about, it enables them to just have a go and gives them strategies to deal effectively with nerves, with stress and with difficulties.

A lot of the children talk to me about how they use it, whether it be for having a filling at the dentist that they were really worried about, how they could cope with that, or sports events inside or outside of school, exams and SATs, and even just for smaller tests, spelling tests etc. that they have during the week. Also with arguments with friends – there's much less teacher intervention needed in our school these days to solve playground arguments because children have got more tools in their tool kit. They might say, 'You know I just need some time to myself, some time to do some breathing' and afterwards they might be able to say, 'Oh I'm sorry about that'. Just a lot less reactivity – it's been a huge impact.

Our teachers say they notice a difference – particularly during transition times, they say it enables the children to settle more quickly. Or perhaps they're coming in from playtime or from somewhere else and are not quite ready to settle straight in to work just yet and a mindfulness practice

(Continued)

(Continued)

enables a class to just settle, to calmly pay attention and concentrate more. Teachers have told me that they notice children using it on the playground – they've seen them doing practices individually and in groups or they can see them doing it for themselves in class.

I had another boy who had a lot of difficulties and it was really affecting his sleep and now he does practices at night time and now he can get to sleep and sleeps all the way through and it's made a huge difference to his sleep. So there's a load of different examples of how children of different age groups use this.

Personal communication, August 2016

Recently I was invited into a primary school in Scotland to introduce mindfulness to a group of 8-year-olds and their teachers. This was a pretty tough area of Edinburgh but the children were very attentive, well behaved – and fun! At the end of the lesson, a little girl came up to me and half whispered 'You know, I have had problems with anxiety'. Unfortunately, even with this tender age group, this is not so uncommon these days.

You will have seen in some of the examples in this chapter that teachers often talk of children using the mindfulness techniques to deal with tests, family arguments, and nervousness. That's been my experience with students too. The 10–11-year-olds I taught in Prague would talk very openly about stress. We are all aware of the rising stress levels young people face these days, and the accompanying rise in mental health issues that are beginning to be serious cause for concern in many countries. The pressures we add to children's lives through the educational system and our test-based approaches are not insignificant and need to be carefully examined.

We have some proven techniques available to us that can help children deal with stress. Perhaps the greatest benefit is the sense of empowerment a child can get from knowing they are not alone, that other people deal with similar issues, and that there are things you can learn to do to take care of yourself. On this front, we – teachers and students – are all trying to cope, as best we can, with some common challenges. This can actually make the work more engaging for us as adults – we are all in this 'being human' together.

If we start to train children early on with age-appropriate exercises, and continue to spiral this awareness training through school, connecting it with other social and emotional learning opportunities, we have the potential to help many young people grow up better equipped to deal with their lives – more resilient and, ultimately, happier. That would indeed be a meaningful shift in the focus of education.

WHAT REALLY MATTERS?

- Being able to sustain our attention when we want or need to.

- Learning to turn towards our experiences and to other people in an open, kind, non-judgemental way.

- Letting children know there are ways to help manage mental health issues.

TRY IT OUT!

For those readers who are working through these Try It Out sections sequentially, we are continuing to use them to build up personal practice, based on content in the chapter. We recommend establishing a personal practice and getting some training before starting to teach mindfulness to students. You will find information on Programmes for Teaching Mindfulness to Students at the end of this section.

- If you didn't watch the Richard Burnett TEDx video, have a look at it now (www.youtube.com/watch?v=6mlk6xD_xAQ).

Watch it in a quiet space so you can try out the brief exercises in the first 10 minutes. These are often used in the introductory sessions with students.

Consider journaling about your experience of the exercises.

- Try this week to *notice your mind's tendency towards storytelling*, especially noting any recurring stories or patterns that might be driven by the 'negativity bias'. Journaling these inner narratives can sometimes help bring them into perspective.

- *Personal practice***:** Try using these suggestions to help establish a slightly longer, unguided, formal sit.

  o Set yourself up in a quiet space where you won't be interrupted for 15 minutes or so.

  o Set a timer so you don't have to worry about when to finish (there's an app called *Insight Timer* that has good bells and interval bells that might help).

  o Establish a posture that's conducive to maintaining a relaxed, alert presence and that allows you to breathe easily.

  o Settle your attention by noticing the physical sensations of the lower half of the body sitting here.

(Continued)

(Continued)

- o Gently expand your attention to notice breath coming in and out of the body, or any expansion and contraction in the body connected with breathing.

- o Aim to sustain your attention on the movement of breath as best you can.

- o Know that the mind will wander away and you will find yourself caught up in thinking.

- o When you notice this has happened, gently, firmly, patiently bring your attention back to the anchor of your breath (or you may prefer to use listening to sounds or sensing the physical sensations of the body as present moment anchors).

- o When the bell ends the session, take a moment to notice how you feel, notice the room and gently stretch and move back, with awareness, into your day.

- Don't be discouraged by a restless mind – that's one of the reasons we train in this way. A single pointed focus that can anchor the attention leads to a closer awareness of the nature of the wandering mind.

- Remember the importance of treating yourself with kindness when you feel tired, uncomfortable, fidgety, frustrated or like you 'just can't do this'!

PROGRAMMES FOR TEACHING MINDFULNESS TO STUDENTS

(adapted with permission from www.discovermindfulness.ca)

The Mindfulness in Schools Project

'.b' for Teens [dot-be] stands for 'Stop, Breathe and Be!' and is a set of 10 lessons designed for youth ages 11–18, each teaching a distinct mindfulness skill in ways that engage young minds.

Similar to '.b', Paws b is designed for ages 7–11, and provides a programme of six 1-hour lessons, or twelve 30-minute lessons.

The Teach .b Certification Course is a 4-day course, and the Paws b Certification Course is a 3-day course. Prerequisites for both include having taken a validated 8-week secular mindfulness course for yourself and at least 6 months of daily practice.

See www.mindfulnessinschools.org.

Mindful Schools

Mindful Educator Essentials (6 weeks online) teaches participants to integrate mindfulness into their work with youth using the K-12 Mindful Schools Curriculum. It provides K-5 curriculum (30 modules for ages 5-12) and Middle and High School curriculum (25 modules for ages 12-17).

Mindfulness Fundamentals (6 weeks online) is a pre-requisite for the Eductaor Essentials course and helps participants establish a personal mindfulness practice.

Mindful Leader (1 year certification, 2 in-person retreat, and 10 months online) is an established mindfulness practice of at least 2 years and completion of Mindfulness Fundamentals and Educator Essentials courses are prerequisites for this course. The year-long certification programme is for dedicated practitioners in the field of mental health and education who are looking to receive an in-depth curricula-based training in becoming a skilful mindfulness teacher for young people. The course involves two week-long summer retreats (in the USA) that bookend the year, and 10 months of online learning.
    See www.mindfulschools.org.

A Still Quiet Place

(10 weeks online) Designed for K-12/secondary educators and allied professionals who are interested in offering mindfulness to children and adolescents to support them in developing their natural capacities for focused attention, engaged learning, emotional fluency, respectful communication, and compassionate action.
    See www.stillquietplace.com.

Mindfulness Based Stress Reduction for Teens (MBSR-T) (10-weeks online) This mindfulness-based stress reduction for teens programme offers an intensive training for professionals interested in helping stressed adolescents find relief and clarity.
    See www.stressedteens.com.

Inward Bound Mindfulness Education (iBme)

Offers a year-long certification programme in teaching mindfulness to adolescents; iBme's *Mindfulness Teacher Training* will prepare educators to implement an in-depth mindfulness curriculum in high schools, colleges and other youth settings. Participants will learn mindfulness practices developed for adolescents and the skills to be effective mindful mentors. The certification combines in-person retreats (in the USA) with online learning.
    See www.ibme.info.

Mindfulness Without Borders

This two-level series is for educators and professionals interested in the concepts of mindfulness, social-emotional learning and teaching strategies of the research-based Mindfulness Ambassador Council youth programme.

- *Level One, Mindful 365* includes five online classes that explore the core concepts of mindfulness and social-emotional learning as they relate to self-awareness, self-management, social awareness, attention, and stress management.
- *Level Two* includes seven online classes that provide specific instruction on the Mindfulness Ambassador Council (MAC), a 12-week intervention that addresses the strategies youth need to support their healthy development. Skills tied to this programme include focused attention, emotion and behaviour regulation, perspective taking, critical thinking and stress management.

See www.mindfulnesswithoutborders.org

Learning to BREATHE (L2B)

A mindfulness-based curriculum for adolescents created for classroom or group settings. This curriculum is intended to strengthen attention and emotional regulation, cultivate wholesome emotions like gratitude and compassion, expand the repertoire of stress management skills, and help participants integrate mindfulness into daily life. Each lesson includes age-appropriate discussion, activities and opportunities to practice mindfulness in a group setting.
See www.learning2breathe.org.

MindUP™

A research-based training programme for educators and children. This programme is composed of 15 lessons based in neuroscience. Students learn to self-regulate behaviour and mindfully engage in focused concentration required for academic success. MindUP™ lessons align with all USA state standards including Common Core and support improved academic performance while enhancing perspective taking, empathy and kindness as well as fostering complex problem-solving skills. There are curriculum guides for K-2, 3-5 and 6-8.
See www.mindup.org.

InnerKids

Teaches age-appropriate, secular activities that develop the ABCs of Attention, Balance and Compassion for youth, ages pre-kindergarten through young adult. InnerKids strengthens and supports how educators communicate and teach with activities that develop greater mind–body awareness, and compassionate life skills as well as helping manage stress.
See www.susankaisergreenland.com.

Teach, Breathe, Learn

(4 weeks online) Equips participants with the skills and confidence to effectively integrate mindfulness and social and emotional learning (SEL) into their own teaching practice and leads professional learning engagements grounded in mindfulness and SEL. The course consists of a weekly 90-minute webinar with opportunities for coaching and support.

See www.teachbreathelearn.com

FURTHER READING AND RESOURCES

Kaiser-Greenland, S. (2010) *The Mindful Child: How to Help Your Kids Manage Stress, Become Happier, Kinder and More Compassionate*. New York: Free Press.

Full of great stories and wisdom with lots of ideas for activities. Especially useful for primary/elementary age children.

Rechstaffen, D. (2014) *The Way of Mindful Education: Cultivating Well-being in Teachers and Students*. New York: Norton.

This is a wonderful resource for supporting teachers in developing their own practice and includes many practical ideas for bringing mindfulness into the classroom.

Jennings, P. (2015) *Mindfulness for Teachers: Simple Skills for Peace and Productivity in the Classroom*. New York: Norton.

A highly regarded practical guide for teachers to help with stress management, understand the research supporting mindfulness and discover ways to impact teaching and learning.

Srinivasan, M. (2014) *Teach, Breathe, Learn: Mindfulness In and Out of the Classroom*. Berkeley, CA: Parallax.

A warm and personal guide for teachers that includes a detailed curriculum for introducing mindfulness to students and draws on the work and wisdom of Thich Nhat Hanh.

Saltzman, A. (2014) *A Still Quiet Place: A Mindfulness Program for Teaching Children and Adolescents to Ease Stress and Difficult Emotions*. Oakland, CA: New Harbinger.

An MBSR-based programme for children and adolescents with excellent first-hand guidance based on Dr Saltzman's experience of working with children.

Hanh, T.N. and Weare, K. (2017) *Happy Teachers Change the World: A guide for cultivating mindfulness in education*. Berkeley, CA: Parallax.

This is the first official, authoritative manual of the Thich Nhat Hanh/Plum Village approach to mindfulness in education. It contains step by step instructions for the core practices, guidance from educators on how these practices work and impact, and exploration on applying these teachings in teachers' lives, classrooms, schools, universities and communities.

6

Mindfulness, Social-Emotional Learning (SEL) and Wellbeing

This chapter:

→ offers a holistic framework for promoting wellbeing for school communities that supports a coherent vision for teaching academic, social, and emotional skills

→ focuses on contextualising mindfulness training within schools and making connections with other skills and curriculum areas

→ looks at schools that have already begun to 'shift the focus' by combining mindfulness with social-emotional skills development.

Part 1: Situating Mindful Awareness Training in Schools

AUTHENTIC AND CONNECTED

Education has become so structured, so organised and over-packaged that it's easy to forget that schools don't *create* learning.

> *Humans learn* - it's what we do.
>
> Schools are able to exist *because* humans learn.

Throughout my teaching career I have often returned to the message from Schank and Cleave (1995) in their Santa Fe Institute paper 'Natural learning, natural teaching', that schools are not natural places of learning:

> The method people naturally employ to acquire knowledge is largely unsupported by traditional classroom practice. The human mind is better equipped to gather information about the world by operating within it, than by reading about it, hearing lectures on it, or studying abstract models of it.'

Given the somewhat artificial nature of schooling, it is important to keep learning connected to the world beyond the classroom and as authentic as possible. **Authentic** and **connected** became watchwords for me as a school principal when looking at curriculum development, project work and subject integration. Keeping learning real and in touch with the needs and interests of the learner are essential elements for engaged learning. This need for authenticity and connection applies just as much, if not more, when we consider including our inner lives and our hearts in learning. When we explicitly include and value the broader developmental needs and experiences of the learner, we bring schooling closer to the natural propensities of human learning - and we make it more relevant.

A FRAMEWORK FOR WELLBEING

Training **mindfulness** skills in schools has greater relevance when it is situated in the context of teaching **social and emotional** skills, which in turn can be housed within the broader framework of enhancing **wellbeing** (see Figure 6.1). Mindful awareness training helps build attention, emotional regulation and related capacities that underlie a range of social, emotional and academic skills.

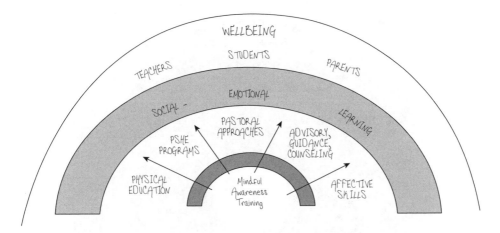

Figure 6.1 A framework for mindfulness, social and emotional skills, and wellbeing in schools

HOW DOES MINDFUL AWARENESS IMPACT SOCIAL–EMOTIONAL LEARNING?

Mindfulness programmes for children and young people often provide opportunities to connect a growing self-awareness with the practical application of skills in daily life. We begin to see the direct transfer of mindful awareness skills to social and emotional development when, for example, students connect self-awareness with the ability to appreciate different perspectives. They might draw on empathic understanding to try to put themselves in someone else's shoes. Or, in other cases, children may learn to know when to take a breath before reacting to difficult situations, to other people or to inner impulses.

- Mindful awareness training can help strengthen our attention skills, building the capacity to sustain curiosity even where things are difficult or challenging.

- The acquired breathing and grounding techniques can help us to calm and centre, giving us just a little more space and time in which we can choose to respond rather than react.

- The heightened awareness of physical, emotional and mental events can increase self-knowledge, for example in noticing what nourishes us, as well as becoming aware of recurring, self-critical thought patterns that might undermine us.

- Overall this increased self-awareness builds empathy; as we understand more about ourselves, we can relate more to the challenges and perspectives of others.

When considering social and emotional competencies, the categorisation from the Collaborative for Academic Social and Emotional Learning (CASEL) shown in Figure 6.2 is very helpful.

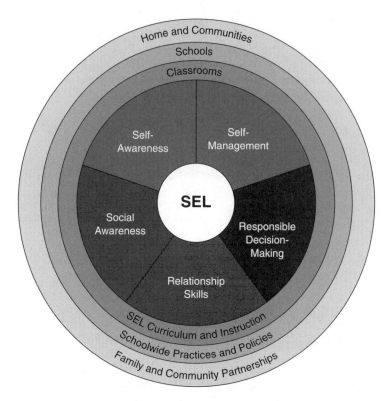

Figure 6.2 Social and emotional learning in schools wheel (CASEL)

The CASEL wheel sets these key competencies of social and emotional learning (SEL) within contexts where students spend their time and organises them into three core areas:

Intrapersonal: self-awareness and self-management

Interpersonal: social awareness and relationship skills

Behavioural/ethical: responsible decision making

When we talk about bringing the heart more into the core of mainstream education through mindfulness, it's these aspects of learning we are focusing on. They are a combination of skills that further self-awareness and self-regulation. We aim through SEL to be able to recognise and articulate our moods and emotions but 'engaging the heart in learning' is also about understanding our feelings and impulses so that we can moderate them when necessary. It's all about balance.

MINDFULNESS–BASED SEL IN ACTION

Experiential training in mindful awareness can build personal understandings and insights that may have immediate relevance and application to our lives. When a

Figure 6.3 Balancing mind, body and heart (reproduced with permission from Petr Dimitrov, International School of Prague)

school puts these affective areas at the heart of its mission, alongside academic development, the core approach to learning has shifted focus and we can see this fruitful alliance of mindfulness with SEL.

Seen through this holistic lens, it becomes more natural to plan curricula and activities that combine the **academic** with the **affective** and the **physical;** that is, a balance of **head, heart** and **body** in learning approaches. One school that has been working to incorporate such a vision into the everyday experience of its students is United World College Thailand.

UNITED WORLD COLLEGE, PHUKET, THAILAND

UWC Thailand is an independent school that follows the International Baccalaureate curricular framework in primary, middle and secondary stages. The school (formerly Phuket International Academy) was founded in 2009 on a combination of mindfulness and social-emotional learning (SEL) within a

(Continued)

(Continued)

child-centred community focusing on inquiry-based education and service learning. Their vision is for students, teachers and families to develop 'A good heart, balanced mind and healthy body' and their mission is:

'Realising our highest human potential

Cultivating genuine happiness

Taking mindful and compassionate action (for peace and a sustainable future)'.

Every day, students from age 3–18 engage in some form of mindful awareness and SEL activity, 'seasoning the day', as they call it, with developmentally appropriate exercises, and weaving affective skills development into their International Baccalaureate programmes at all levels of the school. They even have a Director of SEL and Mindfulness. The founding Director of SEL and Mindfulness, Krysten Fort-Catanese, has shared with us this graphic (see Figure 6.4) that she devised to demonstrate the underpinning of social-emotional competencies by mindful awareness training in the school.

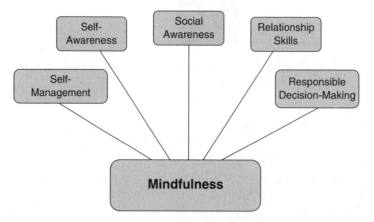

Figure 6.4 Mindfulness-based social and emotional competencies (courtesy of K. Fort-Catanese)

HOLISTIC VISION

The five competencies in Figure 6.4 are from CASEL and it's worth noting here that the title 'C A S E L' combines **Academic** with **Social** and **Emotional Learning**. It's this coherence of outlook, this holistic vision of core skills for learning and for life, that can help transform schooling in the 21st century. We have already witnessed the impact of the information technology revolution on education and it's now time for a parallel movement that prioritises the affective skills, bringing them more into the heart of learning. There are few 'Directors of Mindfulness and SEL' in the world and nowhere near the level of status has been given to this area as has, for example, to IT Leaders, but there are some signs that this is beginning to change.

Even with a school like UWC Thailand that has clarity of vision and a foundation of mindfulness-based SEL (MBSEL), Krysten Fort-Catanese tells us that 'implementing such approaches is always a situation where the tortoise wins the race. With high turnover in the initial years for both administration and teachers at PIA, it has been challenging to create sustainability around SEL and mindfulness at the school. Over time, as stability increased and leadership strengthened, including establishing the role of Director of SEL and Mindfulness, all constituents became invested and involved in the understanding of how to create a culture around such approaches.'

The school has had the benefit of multiple collaborations and consultations with an impressive line-up of key researchers and practitioners in the field, including Susan Kaiser-Greenland, Matthieu Ricard, B. Alan Wallace, Paul Ekman, Richard Davidson, Daniel Rechtschaffen, Joan Halifax and Amy Saltzman. Krysten explains:

> We formed an 'SEL and Mindfulness' committee and eventually the Head of School became invested in order to demonstrate that it starts 'at the top' so to speak. It is now part of the induction that all staff go through an 8-week course in mindfulness so they themselves are living the school mission rather than only focusing on student outcomes. There is also now a higher awareness amongst the faculty that they themselves create the weather in their classrooms.

A 'teacher growth cycle' process helps coordinate required reading for staff on mindfulness in education, as well as using an *IB Learner Profile through SEL Lens* document created by the school, to inform their goals. Teachers provide examples of how they have been of service to others as well as how they have managed their own self-care. 'It has been a long road but integrating systems into the hiring and induction process has had a tremendously positive impact on the school's ongoing commitment to SEL and mindfulness.'

See www.uwcthailand.net/ for further information..

MIND-SHIFT

Creating a new school based around a holistic mission such as UWC Thailand is one thing, but most of us will more often find ourselves trying to bring an altered approach to an already functioning school system, which is quite another thing altogether. Starting a stand-alone mindful awareness or SEL course can be a useful entry point for many schools and it becomes far more effective when you can connect such initiatives with existing programmes and approaches.

It may sometimes be hard to see how this can happen but it is first and foremost a mind-shift. If we re-examine what we are trying to do in schools, 'what really matters', then instead of seeing this as 'yet another thing' to add to our already overcrowded curricula, we can come to truly value such a shift. Then, when we carry out curriculum review processes, we can use a more holistic lens that helps us see the deeper benefits of combining academics and wellbeing. The combination of a deepening dialogue to stimulate such a mind-shift with a gradual, organic change in staff training and curriculum planning can help establish a firm foundation for this work. (Chapter 7 gives some practical examples of how such a process might be undertaken.)

ENLIVENING LEARNING

When we combine mindful awareness training with existing pastoral and social-emotional initiatives in schools, the experiential nature of mindfulness can significantly enliven learning. By emphasising the careful noting of personal experience, this training can help programmes such as character education or anti-bullying interventions become less 'academic' and more visceral – more practical and relevant. Normally classes such as Citizenship or Ethics maintain a more cerebral approach and are in danger of ending up becoming lists of rules for living. But when we recognise and value the inner experience of the learner, then we can begin to help children develop practical moral codes and relevant lessons for life that make sense *from the inside out*. These life lessons then become more memorable, and they stand more chance of being lived, rather than forgotten as soon as the course is over. In this way we begin to teach to parts of the child that ordinary mainstream schooling does not often reach.

Although UWC Thailand is in many ways unique, some other schools are beginning to create high-profile responsibility posts that give significant recognition and leadership to the area of *wellbeing* in schools. Some are overhauling their traditional definition of 'wellbeing' or 'student success' and applying it to the whole school community rather than just as an intervention for struggling students. Whereas the educational adoption of IT was driven by major developments in technology in society, the shift to highlight SEL in schools may need to happen in a more conscious, planned way; it requires sustained effort and willpower to shift this focus.

CHANGING COURSES IN MID–STREAM

Changing the culture of a school is a demanding endeavour and the engagement of teachers is an integral part of the process, so let's look at an example of a school that has been working hard within a well-established culture to try to create something different.

TASIS LONDON

TASIS, The American School In Switzerland, seems oddly named for a school in south-west London, but as one of the most expensive independent boarding schools in the UK they have a tradition of academic challenge and character development. Over the last five years TASIS has been working towards making comprehensive changes that aim to put a much higher emphasis on affective areas within curricular programmes and in extra-curricular activities. Their formula for this work is essentially a combination of positive psychology and mindfulness.

A few years ago I was invited to introduce the TASIS faculty to mindfulness and to the possibility of them being trained in this area, and I have kept track of developments at the school since then. Jason Tait, Head of Upper School Student Life, has led this initiative. Motivated initially by increasing levels of student stress, Jason and some of his colleagues began to try to change the culture of the school to incorporate more centrally the development of core capacities that promote resilience and wellbeing. Overall the intention is for individual students, teachers and the whole school community to be able to *flourish*. Based on research and insights from positive psychology, the aim is not just to cope with stress and deal with adversity, but to be able to study and grow in a fundamentally healthy learning environment that develops the skills, knowledge and competencies necessary for 'a life well-lived'.

Building on aspects of pastoral care and leadership development that were already in place at TASIS, they initially focused on teacher training with all faculty receiving introductions to professional development opportunities in each of three strands: character strengths, resilience and mindfulness. Teachers could then choose one of these areas to focus on in their own personal/professional development and then once trained they could go on to try something out with a class and if it went well, with a whole year group. After five years of teacher training, curriculum planning and initial implementation with students they began to establish a 'framework for flourishing' that would allow them to map and target specific, developmentally appropriate skills for each year group.

As you can see from Figure 6.5, the framework weaves mindfulness, character strengths and resilience work together with a focus on positive emotions and gives students various opportunities to be introduced to, and trained in, these areas.

One of the initial models for this work was Geelong Grammar School in Melbourne, Australia. Jason Tait was already interested in positive psychology and then heard that its founder, Martin Seligman, had spent 6 months at Geelong Grammar helping them develop a whole-school approach based on positive psychology. Jason went there to be trained in 'positive education' and in practical ways of helping a school community become one in which students can truly flourish. I believe this combination of positive psychology with mindfulness has great potential and would make a meaningful alliance. The

(Continued)

(Continued)

excellent work by Carol Dweck (2007) in promoting a 'growth mindset' (now part of the programme at Geelong Grammar) could, I think, create a powerful approach for student development when combined with mindful awareness training in schools.

Whilst schools like TASIS and Geelong traditionally supply students with plenty of challenges, they have not generally, in the past, put much focus on teaching students *how* to deal with those challenges. Often when schools or parents have noticed students struggling with work, for example, the response might have been to give them extra classes or tutors and so sometimes to add even more work to their list. 'Dealing with student stress and anxiety has become a daily issue for us', says Jason, and he believes that the 'flourishing initiative' is a practical way of evolving a school culture that both reduces stress and helps students learn how to manage it.

There have been many challenges along the way for Jason and his colleagues in trying to implement this work, and there continue to be real obstacles to actually getting it fully embedded in the school. Students usually enjoy and appreciate the learning experiences provided, but ironically many will say they don't really have time to spend on it, they are just too busy. Teachers also can be frustrated by wanting to work in these areas but not having time to do so properly. In addition, recent government inspection (OFSTED) reports in the UK may force curriculum time towards other priorities. It takes clear focus, patience and strong intent to maintain these essential developments in schools.

Jason believes that getting teacher buy-in from the start is essential to truly change the culture in a school. 'What I learned from Geelong was that because teachers have not done any of this work in their undergrad or teacher training you have to engage them in a way that's relevant to their own lives.'

Parents are often perceived by teachers and administrators as obstacles to this type of work, but what Jason has found has mirrored my own experience and that of many other schools: 'We started to introduce these ideas at parent coffee meetings, and we have our share of parents who seem focused only on getting their child ready for university, but many of them would also share that their children are sleeping less than five hours a night. And most now say they are glad we are doing this. They support it.'

Jason has helped establish a standing committee on Flourishing for the European Council of International Schools, and in 2016 TASIS hosted the first conference aimed at introducing these approaches to other schools. One thing that is clear is that initiatives which seek to establish a real shift of focus in schools cannot be rushed. They need to grow gradually and organically and cannot just be imposed on teachers. They need time, not least because we are dealing with aspects of human psyche not normally seen as being within the central remit of our schools.

(You can find out more about the Geelong journey here: https://www.ggs.vic.edu.au/School/Positive-Education/What-is-Positive-Education)

Flourishing at TASIS England

The Flourishing Program
This unique program seeks to provide students, teachers, and all members of the community with the opportunity to develop the lifelong skills and habits required to experience a productive life. This is achieved through a combination of feeling good and functioning effectively (Huppert and So, 2011).

Know Yourself
We must know who we are in order to be the best versions of ourselves. We flourish in the face of challenge and opportunity when we have both the knowledge of our own strengths and when we develop the resilience to cope with challenges.

Be Yourself
TASIS believes in the worth of each individual student and his or her potential to make a positive difference in the world. In order to fulfill this potential students must learn to skillfully respond to the present and strive to grow through effort. We must also have the courage to make mistakes and learn from them. In this environment, all members of the community can create more meaningful lives.

Know Yourself	Positive Emotions	
	Engagement	
⟹	Relationships	⟹ Flourish
Be Yourself	Meaning	
	Accomplishment	

TASIS The American School In England
www.tasisengland.org

(Continued)

(Continued)

The Lower School	Flourishing with Core Values	Knowing & Understanding My Feelings
Frog Hollow, Pre-Kindergarten Kindergarten & Grades 1, 2, 3 and 4	Flourishing in the Lower School is based on the Core Virtues program, which encourages habits of the heart and mind. The program objectives are: • To ignite the imagination of the students. • To inspire them to do and to be their best by cultivating character and making positive contributions to the community.	Students in Frog Hollow Nursery, Pre-Kindergarten, and Kindergarten learn about their feelings, including emotions and impulses. They develop an emotional vocabulary and begin to learn how to share their feelings with others. At this stage, there is also a focus on self-control and self-reliance. **Knowing & Liking Myself** Students in first and second grade start to learn about themselves, including what they like about themselves, and they gain an understanding of how to cope with difficulty. They practice skills that develop confidence and begin to learn about identity. **Being My Best Self** Students in third and fourth grade develop skills to help them use their unique strengths to enhance peer relationships and to promote academic success. They explore goal setting, empathy, risk taking, problem solving, and learning styles.
5	**Discovery**	Students in fifth grade learn the vocabulary of Well Being, are introduced to self-care skills, and begin the process of discovering their strengths. The program touches on many aspects of flourishing including zest, mindfulness, resilience, and positive thinking.
6	**Tools for Success**	Sixth grade students are further introduced to the tools for success: grit, self-control, optimism, gratitude, social intelligence, and curiosity. Empathic skills like tolerance and kindness are explored as we build the skills of gratitude, mindfulness, and resilience.
7	**Managing Myself**	Self-control, problem solving, and social-emotional learning are the key topics for seventh grade students. By examining their strengths, students learn to cultivate their best selves and to look for and savor the positive.
8	**Skills for the Future**	After taking the VIA Character Strength Survey, eighth grade students begin to understand how to use their strengths in daily life. They learn about thinking traps and how to combat the effect of stress through mindfulness. Students are also introduced to the concepts of grit and growth mindset.

9	Flourishing in the Face of Challenge & Opportunity	Ninth grade students develop a strong understanding of their own behavior and how they can feel good and function effectively in the face of challenge and opportunity. This module of the program provides students with an in-depth look at the skills of resilience.
10	Developing My Ability to Lead	In the first semester, tenth grade students learn how to take a values/strengths based approach to developing leadership skills. In the second semester, students are introduced to mindfulness and learn how to skillfully and effectively respond to the present.
11	Developing My Potential	Gaining an understanding of grit is the main topic in eleventh grade. Key concepts include: courage, conscientiousness, achievement vs. dependability, setting long-term goals, resilience, optimism, confidence, creativity, and excellence vs. perfection.
12	Flourishing Independently	To support graduates in the next important stage of their lives, the focus is on developing the skills, values, and habits that will allow them to lead meaningful and fulfilling lives beyond TASIS England. Students develop an understanding of how mindfulness will serve them well in a sometimes frantic world.

Figure 6.5   Flourishing at TASIS England

HANDS AROUND THE FLAME

There are many areas of excellence in mainstream education and plenty of good practice to build around, but it's probably the progressive traditions, freed from the pressures of national curricula and testing regimes, that have more often had the space and time to explore more holistic approaches to schooling. They have been, as Michael Fielding (2005) puts it, 'the hands around the flame', and it's the light from these flames that can help illuminate pathways towards a more balanced, more integrated education. We can draw on progressive traditions throughout history and from progressive thinkers like Dewey, Montessori, Steiner and the Reggio Emilia approach which, among others, all have something to offer when we want to explore a more holistic education.

Of course it may be easier for some rich, private, independent schools to trail blaze a shifting of focus in education in an area such as mindfulness, but some visionary state schools are also 'lighting the lamps' of holistic schooling in working towards becoming more mindful school communities. We have already seen how mindfulness has been embedded into the curriculum in ordinary primary schools in the UK, and how this has begun to change the culture of those schools. Stanley Grove primary in Manchester is an example of a school that, having successfully established mindfulness for students and teachers, is now aiming to become a more 'mindful school'.

STANLEY GROVE PRIMARY SCHOOL, MANCHESTER, UK

Amy Footman led the mindfulness initiative whilst she was Deputy Head and is aware that now, as Head of School, she wants to continue to foster the growth of mindfulness but needs to maintain a balanced approach. Although over half of the staff have now taken a full adult course for themselves, there is no obligation to train in or teach mindfulness. Mindfulness classes are taught as part of the Personal, Social and Health Education (PSHE) curriculum and Amy would now like to establish more links between the mindfulness training and other areas of the curriculum and with student behaviour.

'The next big challenge is really widening the change in the ethos around behaviour in the school. It's about the way we have conversations with some pupils who have made a few bad choices. For example, in some situations where I need to become involved after an incident; we don't get many fights these days, but maybe a child has kicked someone else in the playground and then, with those children from Year 4 upwards who have had the training, it would be good to be able to explore what happened with them using vocabulary and imagery from the course.

We have made some time-out tables where they might go and sit for a few minutes and then be ready to talk about what was happening. We have made them more about reflection spaces rather than facing the wall and perhaps feeling humiliated. There is a display around those areas about connecting with how you are feeling, about what the body is telling you, about connecting with positive feelings or memories, a reminder to do a breathing practice etc.

So to make it part of the culture of the school that helps students and teachers manage behaviour, we then need to have those conversations with students in these situations around their thoughts and feelings and help them tune in to their present moment experience in order to understand better what's going on and to learn and grow from it.'

TIME AND SPACE

For many schools with overcrowded curricula and days that are already too busy, the idea of bringing in yet another new area of focus can make it seem difficult to even get started. But here's the thing: *when we begin to allocate time and space to the affective aspects of life and learning, academic achievement rates go up.*

A significant meta-analysis (Durlak et al., 2011) looked at three decades of social and emotional initiatives in the USA and found that, when schools dedicate time to effective social and emotional programmes, 'Students with training in social-emotional learning gained an average of 11 percentile points on standardized test scores compared with students who did not receive the training'. This is, of course, in addition to observed improvements in the behaviours that the interventions were targeting, such as character education, anti-bullying and so on.

The neural pathways in the brain that deal with stress are the same ones that are used for learning. Schools are realising that they have to help kids understand their feelings and manage them effectively. We ... want our kids to achieve more academically, but we can't do this if our kids aren't emotionally healthy.'

Mark Bracket, Director of the Yale Center for Emotional Intelligence, USA (Scelfo, 2015)

In recent years, recognition of the importance of fostering emotional health in the education system has begun to appear in some countries at national level. Singapore regularly tops global league tables that compare students' academic capacities, but a change has been made to refocus on affective skills (using the five CASEL core competencies) and to put them at the core of their educational objectives. This change is in line with a belief in the importance of people skills for the economy as well as in building a harmonious society, and will ensure that all children take part in SEL activities throughout their school journey.

In the USA, where the SEL movement has gathered significant momentum, a National Commission on Social Emotional and Academic Development has been established at the Aspen Institute:

From the schoolhouse to the state house, we have emphasized the academic skills our students need. But overwhelming evidence demands that we complement the focus on academics with the development of the social and emotional skills and competencies that are equally essential for students to thrive in school, career, and life.

The National Commission intends to spark the most important conversation about K-12 education that we have had in a generation – examining the very essence of what constitutes success in our schools. Drawing from research and promising practices, the Commission will explore how to make social, emotional, and academic development (SEAD) part of the fabric of every school. (Aspen Institute, 2016)

Walter Isaacson, President and CEO of the Aspen Institute, summarises the significance of this effort to shift the focus in schools thus: 'We know from human history and the latest learning science that success comes from a combination of academic knowledge and the ability to work with others. We need public education to reflect this' (Aspen Institute, 2016).

MARK GREENBERG, PENNSYLVANIA STATE UNIVERSITY, USA

One of the leading figures in SEL development in the USA is Professor Mark Greenberg from Pennsylvania State University. Based on over 30 years' experience as a psychologist and researcher, Greenberg has developed a deep understanding of the value of social and emotional competencies. Commenting on a study he co-authored that found significant

(Continued)

(Continued)

correlation between social competency in kindergarten and success in adult life, Greenberg said,

> this tells us that the skills underlying what we're testing – getting along with others, making friendships – really are master skills that affect all aspects of life. (Scelfo, 2015).

Despite his background in this area, Greenberg was nevertheless surprised by how clearly the results in this study showed that early social competencies outweighed social class, family circumstances and early academic achievement in predicting wellbeing in later life.

Greenberg has made practical use of his academic and professional experiences by co-developing, with Carol Kusché, a very successful SEL programme for primary schools. The PATHS (Promoting Alternative Thinking Strategies) curriculum is used in schools in various countries, including Northern Ireland and Israel. A series of research trials have shown PATHS to increase healthy student development, classroom engagement and learning, and to reduce behavioural and emotional problems in a wide variety of pre-school and primary school settings.

Greenberg suggests that, when considering the overall value of SEL,

> It's not just about how you feel, but how are you going to solve a problem, whether it's an academic problem or a peer problem or a relationship problem with a parent. The ability to get along with others is really the glue of healthy human development. (Personal correspondence, 2016)

As we have seen, the basic purpose of SEL is to help students and teachers recognise the normal range of positive and negative feelings and to give them tools to slow down and reflect when dealing with conflict, as well as fostering empathy and kindness for self and others. These skills can all be supported and developed though mindful awareness training. Mark Greenberg notes that the work on mindfulness in education fits very well with the larger movement of promoting SEL:

> Mindfulness has the potential to substantially deepen the learning of SEL skills both by sharpening children's attention and awareness as well as by nurturing a deep sense of compassion for others. (Personal correspondence, 2016)

In British Columbia in Canada the educational authorities have been tracking student wellbeing for many years, and in one study (Schonert-Reichl et al., 2015) elementary students taking a mindfulness-based training course (MindUp) saw an average 15 per cent increase in Math scores compared with those taking the regular SEL programme. Other gains were noted in enhanced cognitive control, stress reduction, and improved wellbeing and social interactions.

This is not so surprising when you think about it: we can't learn deeply or effectively when we are feeling insecure or distracted by inner turmoil. Psychologist and author Daniel Goleman says that he came to realise that adding attention training to SEL is an excellent way of 'boosting neural circuitry at the heart of emotional intelligence' (2013: 194). He believes that mindful awareness training, especially when combined into embedded SEL programmes, can play a significant role in helping students develop the key function of improved executive control. Linda Lantieri, Director of the Inner Resilience programme, supports this saying,

> 'I've done SEL for years [but] when I added the mindfulness I saw a dramatically quicker embodiment of calming ability and the readiness to learn. It happens at earlier ages, and earlier in the school year. We lay a foundation of self-awareness and self-management on which you can scaffold the other SEL skills like active listening, identifying feelings and so on.' (Goleman, 2013: 194)

Part 2: Mindfulness–Based SEL in the Classroom – Practical Examples

In my own experience as teacher and administrator I have been fortunate to be able to work in schools where there has usually been the scope to focus on social and emotional aspects of learning. In the UK, in Bradford schools, as an ESL (English as a Second Language) teacher working with mainly immigrant communities in some pretty poor urban areas, the need to engage students and teachers and build emotional investment in their learning and teaching was a key factor. In Tanzania, my school was small and well-rooted in the parent community and we had the parents' respect and trust so that when we gave attention to aspects of learning other than just getting high grades, the parents were able to support us and the school really did flourish. In the Czech Republic, I was the Middle School (11-14 years) Principal at the International School of Prague (ISP) for 10 years, and I share below three concrete examples of using mindfulness in this context to support and enhance social and emotional aspects of learning, focusing especially here on one key social skill – listening.

EXAMPLE 1 – FACILITATING DEEPER CONNECTIONS

We expanded the ISP Advisory programme (equivalent to a tutor group or pastoral programme) so that teachers spent 40 minutes every other day with a small group of students, focusing on organisational skills, relationship building and reflection. The Grade 8 (13-14-year-olds) Advisory Team in Prague established a rotation focus for their sessions using Czech terms that characterise three different styles. *Niterne* was all about individual 'internal' work (e.g. journaling or reflecting); *Meza Nami* classes focused on sharing things 'between us' and would normally involve pair work or sharing with the advisory group; and *Spolecne* was when group activities, often the whole grade 'all together', would take centre stage. The advisors had this set-up working well (see Figure 6.6) and were used to creating

NITERNĚ   MEZI NÁMI   SPOLEČNĚ

Figure 6.6 International School of Prague grade 8 advisory rotation (reproduced with permission from Petr Dimitrov, ISP)

innovative activities, but they also felt they were lacking in the *Meza Nami* area in terms of more formal approaches to building relationships and so they asked for some input.

Just by chance, a few months earlier, I had been at the Central and Eastern European Schools Association conference and on the last session of the last day, I ended up going to a workshop about facilitating deeper connections between students. I didn't really know what this would entail and the workshop was almost empty (only three of us from two schools attending), but it turned out to be one of the best sessions of the conference. That 45-minute input was to provide us with the scaffolding for some dynamic work that still continues in the school many years later.

The presenter was Catherine Ottaviano, the middle school (11–14-year-olds) Counsellor at the American International School of Bucharest (AISB). Cathy and her High School counselling colleague Andy Mennick had identified a divide between the host country (Romanian) students and the rest of the international student body leading to less social integration within the school. Their response was to begin an advisory class that drew on the work of Rachel Kessler who seems to have had an extraordinary gift for understanding and meeting the needs of teenagers. Her book *The Soul of Education* (2000) is a jewel – more of an approach than a programme, but full of meaningful insights into what teenagers yearn for, and ideas for dynamic and practical ways of moving towards meeting those needs.

We took the AISB Kessler-based work and adapted it to our 8th grade needs in Prague. Most of our grade 8 students had already received training in mindfulness so they had experienced sitting in silence together and had learnt how to focus their attention. We used mindful cues to help them settle into this different type of advisory session and then to promote deeper listening. For each of these special sessions, students would arrive to find a space cleared on the floor, covered with a cloth or blanket and cushions for them to sit on (signalling that this would not be your average 40-minute class).

On some occasions students would have been asked to bring in an artefact from home the day before, something that was 'important to you'. The assembled objects would be laid out ready in the centre of the class (including one from the teacher) and after a few moments of mindful settling to transition into this differ-ent space, one student would start by asking 'What's this?' and the owner would pick up the object and speak for a few minutes or so about why it was important to them. During this time, no one else spoke: the rest of the group practised atten-tive listening, creating a space into which the speaker could speak and be fully heard. When the student finished speaking there would be no comment, just a 'Thank you' from the teacher and then on to the next object. At the end of the session time would be devoted to a more open conversation where students could ask each other more questions or make further comments about their own object or about others'. The focus of the sharing sessions varied each time and every activity involved some kind of artwork, ritual or artefact, for example decorating a paper plate to illustrate 'What I bring to the table' or closing the year with a ritual burning of artwork symbolising 'Things I want to leave behind in middle school'.

The change in the quality of speaking and listening in these sessions was pal-pable. Their mindfulness training supported the students' ability to listen deeply to each other. They would often say that at first they felt a bit uncomfortable but then they began to really appreciate these sessions: 'I learned something about my friend that I have never heard her talk about before' or 'I understand a bit more now about why he behaves the way he does, and I don't get so annoyed by it'. We took care to consider questions of confidentiality, and we created not only a safe space within the sessions but also agreements about respecting others' rights and feelings in not discussing content outside the classes.

What I learned from this and, and from reading Rachel Kessler, was that young people *do* respond well to rituals and opportunities for deeper connection – far better than I would have imagined – and that teenagers, just like their younger primary age counterparts, *do* want, and even yearn, to share. In some ways this activity is similar to circle time in primary school – the difference is that creating the conditions for deeper sharing with teenagers requires much more careful and sensitive facilitation: the conditions have to be just right for students to feel secure enough at this stage to share more openly and to *really* listen to each other.

In Bucharest all sessions in the High School had been led by counsellors, but in Prague we decided to train the advisors to facilitate the sessions themselves. My co-trainer, Amy Burke, and I would meet with the group of teachers a week or so in advance of these special activities and go through the exercises with them in real time (sitting on the floor, bringing in an artefact etc.) so that they had the chance to get a feel for the importance of 'holding the space' that would be required for this to work well, and for checking over the logistics of the activity.

An important and unforeseen by-product of this work was that this process cre-ated a deeper bonding between the advisory teachers themselves. I had noticed that I really enjoyed working with this group, and as Principal and colleague I felt very accepted by them. But it was not until one of the teachers spoke up in our final session that I was able to credit this feeling to the group-work training ses-sions. The teacher had previously been at a very good international school with a well-developed advisory system. She had been there for many years but told us that, after just a few months working with the grade 8 team, she felt closer to this group of teachers than she had felt in her time at the previous school, and she attributed this to those training sessions. We didn't necessarily always share on a deep level, but even so this showed that it does not take so much for us to be able to shift the focus of a busy school day to contain some deeper moments of authentic connection, moments that we just don't normally find the time and space for. These connections can really improve our working relationships and make both formal and informal collaboration more effective in schools.

Council

The format we used in the sessions for deepening dialogue was based on council practice, which is derived from the traditions of indigenous peoples. You can see a lovely video about council practice in schools at www.youtube.com/watch?v=fK Sh73dO49s&ab_channel=ojaifoundation. (*Note:* The Ojai Foundation's Council in Schools section offers comprehensive training in facilitating council practice.)

Once they got the hang of it, some teachers found that council could be used in different situations (e.g. in Social Studies discussions or literature reviews) wherever we wanted to help our students really listen to each other. The same applies to MBSEL approaches in general – they don't have to be limited to Advisory, PSHE or Pastoral classes. Although mindful awareness and SEL skills can be taught as discrete courses, an emphasis on affective skills can also permeate all areas of the curriculum, and once you begin to see the value of combining the head and the heart in learning you will be able to find many opportunities to apply these skills in a wide range of contexts. There are of course natural links between physical education, health education and awareness of mind, body and emotions, but there are also many other ways of reinforcing a more balanced approach to learning.

There is a beautiful quote by Joe Provisor, Founder of Council in Schools in the video mentioned earlier:

> 'Fundamentally, Council is a practice that supports the basic skills of listening and speaking, and these underlie the skills of reading and writing.
>
> What is reading but listening from the heart to the story of another?
>
> And what is writing but feeling that you have a story to tell in the listening of others?
>
> In this way, Council is the basis of all other academic skills.'

And it's true – traditional schooling is quick to focus on the analytical and the critical, often at the expense of deeper, more fundamental human capacities and experiences. When an artist or musician or author creates a piece of work, they are tapping into these qualities. A writer writes a meaningful story from the heart and we feel its message when we read. But what do we do with it in schools? We jump straight to analysing it, exercising our critical skills – which are highly important skills, yes, but do we give equal attention to hearing and valuing the response of the learner to the work? Do we know how to create an emotionally safe learning environment in which readers can register these responses on a deeper, more heartfelt level? Some teachers are very adept at bringing this out in their students, but all too often we are in danger of unintentionally sucking the life out of a creative work of art for the sake of a future test. We can understand and appreciate these works of art as stories and experiences given from the heart, and perceived through emotion, as well as through analysis.

Even in less-obviously 'heart-centred' areas such as, for example, science we can help students combine their analytical understanding of the world with a sense of wonder. What is the point for a young person of the detailed knowledge of the cellular process of photosynthesis unless they can also sit under a tree on a summer's day and appreciate the amazing fact that we are here, at just this distance from the Sun, not too hot, not too cold, in sunlight that can enter that filtered leaf and arrive on our bodies at *just* the right temperature, and be able to marvel at the tree taking sustenance from the light right in front of our very eyes, in this moment, now?

Biology, the 'study of life', should mean more to students than memorising cellular processes. Exploring the senses can have an important role to play in science - and the role of our own unique experience should not be overlooked here either - life and learning is not just about stuffing ourselves with known facts but also about feeling, appreciating and understanding - from the inside out.

Psychology, the amazing 'study of the human psyche', and theories about the mind, surely should also be about exploring how our own mind works, especially as it is our instrument for learning. Both my daughters studied Psychology at IB level and one went on to take it as her major at university. Excellent courses yes, but in 5 years of studying the psyche (of others) she was not expected to spend 5 minutes exploring her own.

We are certainly not advocating that schools become introspective places where students engage in endlessly baring their souls to each other, but we need to find a better balance of head and heart in learning. If we bring a more mindful attentiveness to articulating and legitimising our deeper responses, can we infuse learning with more of the humanity that it merits?

EXAMPLE 2 - TRAINING LISTENING IN FOREIGN LANGUAGE CLASSES

One year in Prague I went into every 7th-grade (12-13-year-olds) foreign language class and taught some deep listening skills. Then I visited all the EAL (English as an Additional Language) and SEN (Special Educational Needs) classes so in fact I was able to cover the whole grade. The teachers would prepare a challenging listening activity, for example in Spanish class, distinguishing three different South American accents and noticing any common content. Before starting this I would take the class through a fun mindful listening activity, heightening their auditory awareness and settling their minds in order to ready them for some open, receptive listening. After this preparation they engaged really well with the teacher's listening activity.

The approach I used in these classes was a different type of listening to standard exercises where you have to concentrate hard to be able to interpret what is being said in another language. I based it on my own experiences of language learning.

LANGUAGE LANDSCAPES

'Kevin will never be a linguist.' Those damning words from my French report, age 13 at Chichester High School for Boys, were etched boldly into my memory. For many years I believed it and found that when French colleagues of my dad's came to stay with us my schoolboy French really didn't cut it. Not surprising, given the way they taught us at school. French was pretty much just like all the other subjects, something to be studied and analysed, not exactly a living language you were expected to use or play with. Despite the occasional 'language lab' activity, it was all deadly boring and I learnt very little.

It wasn't until I was 22 that I discovered I can learn languages. But I need to hear them, not just study them in books. I need to be surrounded by the language and immersed in the culture. After 3 months living in Chartres, France, I spoke pretty fluent (if ungrammatical) street French. What I discovered was that if I immersed myself in the culture, almost pretended to 'be French', and was forced to hear and speak the language, then I could indeed pick up the language pretty quickly.

A few years later, on a trip to South America, I hoped my French and basic Latin would give me some foundation for Spanish, but it wasn't until I had spent many hours trying - and failing - to get from the Tijuana bus station to the Tijuana train station on my first day in Mexico that I realised that I actually couldn't speak any Spanish, at least not in a way that anyone could understand.

Two weeks later I was lying on a camp bed on the roof of the Mexican boarding-house I was living in in Mazatlan. My fellow boarders, a group of Mexican college students, were practising some kind of play. Exhausted from being bombarded by a language I couldn't understand and unable to use my own, I lay back and looked at the sky and just let go. I stopped trying to translate everything and just listened to what I was actually hearing. For the first time, I actually *heard* Mexican Spanish. Instead of trying to compare this new 'terrain' with my native language landscape, I was just hearing it, for itself.

From this moment on, having had a glimpse of the overall 'shape' of the language, any bits and pieces I did understand now fitted into a context. At the end of the third week my friends stopped me mid-sentence one evening and said, 'Hey Kevin, what's going on? Last week you couldn't say two words and now you can't stop talking. What happened?!'

In the 'deep listening' activities with language students, the aim was to learn to sometimes be able to let go of grasping at translation and just enjoy the music of a language for itself. I believe when we do this we move into a more mindful 'being mode' and allow the brain to do some of the work on its own, assimilating new sounds into an emerging linguistic landscape. I've tried this activity in other schools, with very young children as well as at IB Diploma Level, and teachers have reported that students really enjoyed it and afterwards would ask for more listening activities.

When training the 7th grade in this approach I would always leave a chime bar as a gift to the class so they could use it any time they wanted to help them drop into silence for a moment. In this way, as well as doing the listening, we were helping students and teachers establish a shared quiet space that they could return to before a listening activity or when doing busy project work. It can be restorative for students to have a moment of quiet from time to time during a class, to come back to a calmer place and then start again from there. This is good for teacher mental-health too!

 CAUTIONARY NOTE - BELLS AND SILENCE

I tend to use chime bars in schools as they are normal school equipment available through music department catalogues, whereas some bells may suggest a more religious implication. It's important, though, not to begin to use a bell or chime bar in place of whatever technique you normally use to get students' attention (e.g. raised hands, counting down from 5, etc.). Keeping the bell for something more 'invitational' means that students can feel more positive about inhabiting a familiar quiet space for a moment - otherwise it can feel like just another control tool. It works much better, of course, when students have been properly trained in shared silence so they know what to expect when a bell is sounded. Some teachers allow students to request a 'mindful moment' and then the requesting student is allowed to ring the bell for the class, which they seem to enjoy doing.

I have seen schools get interested in mindfulness and then jump in too quickly, thinking it's all very simple, initiating a silence in every assembly or ringing bells in classes for quiet times. This can actually turn some kids (and teachers) off the idea of being silent and will only work if the ground has been well-prepared - teachers need to have a background in mindfulness meditation themselves so they can understand that not everyone is feeling calm during a shared silence. Accessing their 'still quiet place' (as Dr Amy Saltzman calls it in her mindfulness programmes for children) makes much more sense when students have been properly trained in visiting that space - and they know that it's OK if sometimes it doesn't feel quiet or still!

EXAMPLE 3 - TRAINING DEEP LISTENING SKILLS FOR GROUP WORK

Getting students in middle and high school to sit quietly and do breathing exercises or feel their feet on the floor may not always be an instant hit with this age group, but I have found that most children and teenagers enjoy the listening activities, especially if you praise their skills. They love to tell you about all the subtle sounds they heard that you didn't.

Sometimes we would take this a step further in Prague and look in more depth with a year group at the importance of listening and of applying listening skills to school and life contexts. I often used to remind my teachers that, while it's easy for us to put children into groups to work together, we may not always explicitly recognise how hard it can be to work collaboratively. Even for us as colleagues, personalities and approaches can, of course, clash. ISP do a lot of project-based learning and this provides plenty of opportunities for students to fall out or to struggle with effective communication. Because collaborative and communicative skills are so important these days, we highlighted a range of group-work and self-management skills that students focused on during these projects, in addition to their academic objectives.

Before getting started the counsellor prepared the students by teaching them some terminology they could use for group work. Can they recognise *roles* they sometimes play in groups? Do they help to *problem solve* or *harmonise* a group? Or do they sometimes *block* or *distract* group efforts? Then I took the whole grade for an afternoon to focus on listening skills. All students had already had an introduction to listening in their language or learning support classes so I was able to jump right into these activities.

Here's a fun way of introducing a focus on listening that I have used many times:

STEP 1 – FEELING HEARD (10–15 MINUTES)

- Pick two volunteers, usually teachers but this can work with students too as long as you choose carefully and make sure you let them know what's coming.

- Stand at the front of the room, a volunteer on either side. Turning to one say. 'Just talk to me for a minute or two about anything that comes to mind for you about working in groups.'

- Start out by paying attention to the speaker then in a short while let them see your focus begin to stray, maybe turning away a little, perhaps stifling (not too discreetly) a yawn, maybe jumping in and throwing out a quick opinion of your own, then looking away again. Keep this going for a short time, even if they struggle to keep their train of thought going.

- After thanking the first volunteer, turn to the second with the same question but this time giving full, quiet attention, eye contact, subtle nods or 'Uh huh's, and when they are done, summarise what they said.

- Before asking the students to give feedback ask the volunteers to share how it felt.

When I ask students what the second person had said, they could usually tell me, but about the first there was little recall. This leads nicely into:

'Have you ever had something you wanted to tell someone but it didn't really seem like they were listening?'

And of course everyone's experienced that.

'And how does that feel?'

Then, in contrast,

> 'Have you ever had the experience of telling someone something important to you and they really listened well?'

> 'How does that feel?'

And all this sets the group up to be ready to reflect on:

> 'What gets in the way of really listening to someone?'

This is actually equivalent to 'What gets in the way of really being present?' Students may come up with ideas such as being distracted by other noises, by thoughts or by pain, feeling uncomfortable, being bored, wanting to tell your own story and so on. These can all be helpful reminders of the challenge of really 'being with' someone. Even the acknowledgement of these obstacles in the moment can help us take a step towards being more present. With older students and teachers the idea of 'trying to fix things' often surfaces, allowing us to explore the power of just being with someone without trying to solve their problems – and also, an understanding of the profound value of simply being able to be heard.

 ## STEP 2 – PAIRS WHISPERING (10–15 MINUTES)

After the 'Feeling Heard' exercise I usually go on to do a 'pairs whispering' activity, using the 'Roles People Play in Groups' vocabulary that the counsellor has already taught the students (for details see the Try It Out section at the end of this chapter).

- Pairs sit shoulder to shoulder, not looking at each other, facing in opposite directions.

- I lead a short guided-listening practice, listening to the sound of the chime bar as it fades away and then to other sounds and silences that fill the space for a minute.

- I then cue them with the chime bar to listen carefully while the first speaker whispers or talks gently about 'How I am in group work'.

- The listener then summarises what was heard. They reverse roles before ending with a final, normal conversation about group work or about how it felt to do this exercise.

This almost always creates a powerful atmosphere in the room, with teachers as well as with students. Of course, once it comes to the free-for-all of group work in a normal class situation the level of dialogue will be quite different. But the teachers can take part in these practice sessions and can remind students of the importance of attentive listening and speaking mindfully. Sometimes they might use a moment of quiet or a Council practice to help deepen the dialogue in a normal class situation. By the end of the project students are able to explain quite articulately to parents at the student-led conferences how their affective skills have developed over the course of the project.

These examples point to how useful and important such skills are in learning, but also in life, especially in a world where it sometimes seems like everyone is talking but nobody is listening. I wish my teachers had known more about the importance of developing emotional intelligence as well as academic capacities when I was at school – I could have applied this training over and over again in my personal life and my work. A more central focus on the affective skills in schools can thus make learning more relevant and also help develop a more balanced learner – and person.

WHAT REALLY MATTERS?

- Recognising that we are social, emotional, intellectual and physical beings and that we need to open ourselves and our schools to honouring the richness of the human spirit in all its forms.

- Finding practical opportunities in schools to develop relevant and meaningful skills and qualities such as deep listening, empathy and compassion.

TRY IT OUT!

For yourself:

- Before trying out listening skills work with students, consider using sounds as an anchoring object for your own regular formal mindful meditation practice.

    o You can look over the guidance below for a sounds meditation or, listen to a recording of it at www.mindwell-education.com.

- Sounds Practice for Teachers (8–10 minutes)

    o Settle into your sit as usual, perhaps using the sensations of the body to help you.

    o Become aware of the breath moving in the body.

    o Allow the eyes to close, or the gaze to lower and soften.

    o When you feel settled and ready to open to sounds, move your attention to the ears and become gently aware of the soundscape surrounding you in this moment.

    o Notice whichever sounds are most apparent to you – sounds from outside the room, or from nearby, or from your body.

    o No need to grab at the sounds, just open yourself to them, allowing them to come to you.

    o When you notice the mind has moved into thought, 'labelling' or telling stories connected with sounds, gently refocus on *the physical sounds themselves*, noticing for example, volume, pitch and texture.

o   Notice the connection between sounds and distance.

o   Notice any moments of silence that may appear.

o   Notice constant sounds, intermittent sounds, subtle sounds.

o   Allow the richness of the soundscape or the spaciousness of the silences to receive your full attention.

o   And when you become aware that the mind has moved off into thoughts, just accept that the mind will wander and gently and firmly, return it to focus on sounds, your anchor in the present moment.

o   Finally, expand your awareness to sense sounds with the whole body for a few moments.

o   Acknowledge any sense of spaciousness that this meditation might bring.

o   And then gently opening the eyes, looking around, still maintaining awareness of sounds as you bring the session to a close.

There are many online listening meditations available online, here is one suggestion: www.contemplativemind.org/audio/MB_Breath_Sound_Meditation.mp3.

With your students:

- Listening Activity (3-5 minutes)

   Consider doing a short listening activity with your students at the start or end of a class, or before an activity that requires a calm focus:

   o   Ask them to sit in a way that they feel comfortable and alert.

   o   Tell them you want to see how good they are at listening.

   o   Perhaps ask them to close their eyes if they feel comfortable (and if not just lower their gaze) so they can give all their attention to listening.

   o   Set a timer for 2 minutes and tell them that during this time, all they need to do is listen quietly and notice what they hear. Join the students in this active listening yourself.

   o   When the time is up, elicit a list from them of all the different sounds they heard (perhaps praise them for being good listeners, underlining sounds they heard that you didn't).

   o   Either now or on a second session in a later class, you could prompt them for more subtle sounds they might notice.

   o   If appropriate, you could ask them to notice how they feel after listening, or to notice how the room feels as the listening practice ends.

(Continued)

(Continued)

- Class Focus On Listening Skills

  If you are interested in bringing more focus to listening skills in your classes, you could try using the activity described on page 136 as a way into starting a dialogue with students about the importance of listening and of being heard.

  - o This focus could be extended to looking at behaviour and roles in group work in a similar way to that described in the chapter. See the following link for Roles People Play in Groups: https://web.stanford.edu/group/resed/resed/staffresources/RM/training/grouproles

  - o Using short listening exercises in any class can help students calm and refocus and may sometimes attune them to a slightly deeper level of dialogue.

  - o Have fun with listening activities such as these at the Exploratorium Museum: www.exploratorium.edu/listen/online_try.php.

FURTHER READING AND RESOURCES

Edutopia (www.edutopia.org) is a great source for ideas and examples of inquiry-based project work and using SEL in schools.

Kessler, R. (2000) *The Soul of Education: Helping Students Find Connection, Compassion and Character At School*. Alexandria, VA: ASCD.

A wonderful guide to working with adolescents that speaks to the spirit of youth, connection and learning.

Elias, M. and Zins, J.E. (1997) *Promoting Social and Emotional Learning: Guidelines for Educators*. Alexandria, VA: ASCD.

An early but influential guide to SEL in the 21st century from a team of writers and researchers working with the Collaborative for the Advancement of Social and Emotional Learning.

Seligman, M. (2011) *Flourish: A Visionary New Understanding of Happiness and Well-being*. New York: Free Press.

An accessible book full of entertaining stories that also serves as a helpful introduction to the science and application of positive psychology.

Lantieri, L. (2008) *Building Emotional Intelligence*. Boulder, CO: Sounds True.

Practical exercises that combine SEL with mindfulness to help children mange stress and build resilience and empathy.

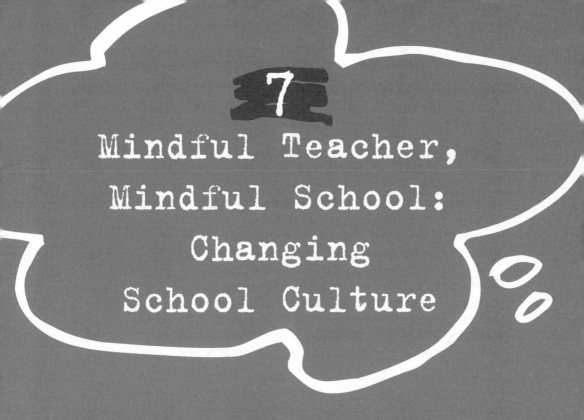

7

Mindful Teacher, Mindful School: Changing School Culture

This chapter:

➢ considers some of the practical and organisational issues of bringing mindful awareness training and a greater emphasis on the affective skills into schools

➢ addresses school leaders interested in supporting these developments

➢ explores examples of practical ways of changing the culture of a school, including working with parents.

Adding a mindfulness course for students into the curriculum can be a good way to get things started in a school, but if we really want to start to shift the focus of education then we stand a much greater chance of stimulating sustainable change when we take our time to look holistically at connecting with existing initiatives and approaches and building a more coherent framework. As we saw in Chapter 6, situating mindful awareness training within the context of existing pastoral approaches and social and emotional programmes can be an effective first step for schools. Positioning mindfulness and social-emotional learning within a broader school framework of wellbeing - *Mindfulness Based Wellbeing* - takes this a step further and provides an integrated view that can inform future curriculum planning.

An informed focus on wellbeing in schools brings together the need for physical, mental and emotional health. Although there may be a tendency, especially in the media, to jump on developments such as mindfulness as if they are some kind of panacea, we need to keep the idea of balance at the forefront of discussions on wellbeing. Plenty of physical exercise, good nutrition and getting enough sleep are just as important as maintaining positive mental health.

A DIFFERENT DAY

In schools like UWC Thailand that we looked at in Chapter 6, an integrated approach to mindfulness-based social-emotional learning infuses the whole day. When a busy day begins to be punctuated by meaningful moments of shared stillness, the whole emotional atmosphere of a classroom (and a school) changes. This can reduce stress, nourish the soul and - for teachers as well as for students - make the whole experience less of a busy sprint to the end and more of a measured, even savoured, learning experience. In this more mindful way, schools and teachers can provide the moments of rest and recovery that our mind-body systems so desperately need to be able to truly learn and teach all day long. By finding ways to engage the restorative processes of the 'parasympathetic nervous system', teachers model those qualities of calm and inner stability that are needed to counteract the tendency to anxiety and insecurity which is becoming an almost commonly accepted feature of life in the 21st century.

PACING CHANGE

When looking at new initiatives in schools we need to foster change in a broad-minded, thoughtful and sensitive way. Rather than trying to force new ideas onto a school community, a healthier approach is to consider this as the beginning of a dialogue with faculty, administrators, support staff, students and parents. If we are concerned with creating flourishing communities where the aim is improving wellbeing, then a good place to start is by involving any interested parties in a reflective exploration of the issues. At the end of introductory retreats and mindful awareness training courses we often advise teachers who may be fired up and enthusiastic to take a breath and take a few steps back before they start to introduce their ideas to colleagues and students. I discovered at my own cost that when you push, you inevitably get push-back. My first few years of teaching mindfulness in my own school were not easy, particularly with my colleagues on the leadership team where I was quite often the butt of some mild mockery. Even with my own faculty I think there were times when some teachers were worried I might be off on some strange personal odyssey.

At that time I could find no other teachers doing this work in international schools, apart from one, in the American Embassy school in Delhi, who was teaching a home-grown mindfulness course to her 6th-grade (11-year-old) Health students. This was Meena Srinivasan, who later wrote the book *Teach, Breathe, Learn* (2014) based on her experience in India. She offers teachers a beautiful Thich Nhat Hanh inspired curriculum that includes many lovely comments and insights from her students showing how touched they were by these simple heart-based classes. Although Meena was very much a trailblazer in teaching mindfulness to students, she was working in a relatively supportive context. The Embassy school was an American school with a twist, perhaps due to its context in India – many teachers were practising meditators and there was a supportive community of like-minded teachers.

> When you feel you are a lone voice in a school it can be tough at first.

Getting the balance right between trying to bring change and provoking push-back is not easy. Fortunately, at the time I when I was experiencing difficulty in getting mindfulness started in my own school, I was taking Amy Saltzman's excellent online teacher training course, *Still Quiet Place* (a mindfulness programme for children and adolescents). I was prone to getting excited and evangelising about mindfulness at my school then getting push-back from colleagues; this caused me to hesitate and close down for a while. Amy gave me some great advice based on her understanding of martial arts. She counselled me to consider a more composed movement, similar to Aikido or Tai Chi where you are able to maintain your centre of balance and advance, retreat or step aside as called for in any given moment. That really helped – I lessened my efforts to persuade the rest of the school to take this on and focused more on my own practice, enjoying bringing mindfulness training to the middle school students who signed up for my courses, as well as the teachers that chose to do the same.

Gradually things started to change – the High School (14-18-year-olds) Principal was exploring meditation and yoga for herself at that time. Along with the high school counsellors, she was concerned with the students' physical, mental and emotional state while handling the challenges of the intense International Baccalaureate Diploma-based curriculum. It was encouraging when students chose to take short-term optional mindfulness programmes. Soon some high-school teachers were trained in teaching mindfulness and the high-school programme then introduced a series of mindfulness lessons for all grade 11 (17-year-old) students.

There was, though, still a problem with the whole mindfulness initiative being too identified with me personally. I have talked to other 'early adopters' about trying to get beyond a common perception such as 'that's Kevin's thing'. Perhaps this is inevitable with these types of initiatives that aren't quite your average professional development training. Tim Parks, author of *Teach Us to Sit Still* (2010), said in relation to mindfulness in education 'Feeling your feet on the floor is a radical act in the classroom'. Perhaps in a decade or so it will seem perfectly normal, but for the time being this can feel like an unusual direction for schools to take and it is important to proceed slowly and sensitively.

It's important also to recognise that introducing mindfulness courses can be a practical challenge for schools. It requires teachers to develop their own practice and get trained up; if staff then move on, they take their expertise with them. To become sustainable, this type of change needs a shift in the school culture and on-going professional development opportunities.

What I had hoped for in Prague was that we would carry out a whole-school holistic review of health and wellbeing, similar to the one outlined in Chapter 6 at TASIS, but unfortunately this didn't happen in my time there. It is important to accept that the type of changes we may hope for in schools can take a long time to grow and become embedded. Sometimes, the conditions might already be in place for swift changes to occur. More often, we need patience and clarity of intent. Even where schools seem resistant to change, individual efforts count – in fact, they are the most important elements in sowing seeds for future change. New ideas that challenge our assumptions about the nature of schooling sometimes have to spiral around and be heard several times, from different sources, before they can stick.

If you don't have a supportive environment in your workplace right now, you can still focus on the shift within yourself and let things grow organically. When colleagues notice changes in you and your teaching or in your students, this can have a powerful impact on them. In fact, this is often *the* most powerful way of initiating change in this area.

CHANGING SCHOOL CULTURE: THEORY AND PRACTICE

When I work with a school community I often do an introduction along the lines of a condensed version of Chapter 1, taking care to provide experiential entry points for everyone. I try to present this in an inclusive, down-to-earth manner and to normalise a wide range of potential reactions and perspectives. I find that using a reflective exercise around that question 'What do we really want for our children?' helps create a good quality of dialogue as well as a powerful starting point that can identify common values amongst a wide range of parents and teachers.

We have seen examples of some schools that have made significant progress in making a focus on affective skills central to their work, but in terms of mindfulness-based wellbeing in education, we are all still very much at the beginning – there are not so many established models out there for us to look to.

As we have just seen, in my school in Prague we weren't able to firmly establish mindfulness throughout the whole school within a holistic framework of wellbeing in the way I would have liked to, and this brings us to the important question of the challenge of changing cultures in schools.

HOW CAN WE EFFECTIVELY SHIFT THE FOCUS OF A SCHOOL?

School systems are notoriously resistant to change, so it's important to understand a little about why that is so. I will draw here on an example of culture shift from working with the middle school (11–14 years) faculty at the International School of Prague (ISP).

Please note that this example is not about mindfulness per se but, as you will see, there are connections between the approach I outline and the conditions necessary to make deep change in schools (such as a shift in focus towards seeing wellbeing and affective skills as central concerns).

In particular, there are useful parallels in this example with the themes of:

- building self-awareness
- finding personal engagement and entry points for teachers and parents
- preparing the ground through deep listening and productive dialogue.

INTERNATIONAL SCHOOL OF PRAGUE. MIDDLE SCHOOL. CZECH REPUBLIC

It was a real delight, when I arrived at ISP Middle School, to find such a dynamic team of educators: hard-working, student-centred and dedicated to making our school the best that it could be. We were very well resourced, with a forward-looking administration and while the parent community may have been quite conservative in their views on education, I found that if you prepared the ground well and included them in the discussion, they would generally be supportive - even where changes may have gone against some of their instinctive ideas about schooling.

However, after a few years in the job, despite overall being happy with the quality of the education we were offering, I began to feel a bit frustrated: given the situation I've just described and my intention to move us away from the traditional American style education that I had inherited at the school, how come we were still doing more or less the same old thing? Wasn't it our responsibility, given such a privileged position and all those resources, to produce something more progressive, more radical?

(Continued)

(Continued)

It was then that I came upon the work of Peter Senge, especially his influential book *The Fifth Discipline* (1990), which I found to be highly relevant to our needs. We used some of his ideas and techniques directly in our re-visioning of the middle school. I notice now that almost every page of my copy of *The Fifth Discipline* is underlined or dog-eared – so much seemed to be directly applicable to schools even though it was primarily written for the business world. Two key factors were of particular relevance to our situation:

- First, the value of developing a deeper dialogue, not just the normal brainstorm and discussion that often precede curriculum development. Many well-intended school reforms end up petering out if teachers are not fully engaged in a deeper way with the process from the start and even inspired programmes will fail if they become superficial box-ticking exercises.

  (One example of this is the Social-Emotional Aspects of Learning (SEAL) programme in the UK. This important programme, which is still used today in pockets in the UK and other countries, failed to find the footing it deserved because of lack of investment in teacher implementation.)

- Second, the importance of surfacing our own assumptions about the system we are operating in. Even though we may all have positive ideas about how things should or could be, if we don't examine our underlying belief systems then we can't dig deep enough to prevent new ideas ending up replicating old systems. This is a perennial and frustrating aspect of much school reform and often comes back to how we as teachers can sometimes unconsciously subvert change initiatives, often because deep down we don't believe in them (and often for good reason).

Peter Senge has spent most of his time working in industry and global management, but he has also taken a strong interest in education. His great gift has been to help others understand the complexities of systems thinking and how to apply these insights on a practical level to promote deep change. He also co-wrote a book called *Schools that Learn* (2000) and we used this book to help us re-examine our priorities in the middle school. (You can see Senge talking about the future of education in this 5-minute video: http://schoolsthatlearn.com/resources/)

We had already started to consider the question 'What really matters in middle school?' and we had general agreement amongst the faculty that change was desirable. At that time there were so many interesting curriculum initiatives coming our way that we needed to be discerning about what we took on. Some of these ideas came through teachers' experience of their previous schools or from conferences and trainings they had attended. Most came from senior management coming back from other schools and conferences inspired with new ideas. It was a time when it seemed like everybody in international schools was rewriting curricula, re-examining their principles of curriculum design and exploring different approaches to learning, especially given the impact of technology. In some ways we were too open to possible changes – in danger of being blown around from one initiative to another, and perhaps making superficial changes without really transforming schooling in the way many of us deep down hoped to.

In schools one factor that gets in the way of change that doesn't apply in industry and business is that we – teachers, administrators, parents – have all been to school and so we all have our own notions (our 'mental models') of what constitutes a good education and what doesn't. But it's only when we surface and compare these assumptions that we can begin to move beyond them and see with greater clarity both 'what is' and 'what is possible'.

We decided to dedicate a full professional development day to reviewing our position in middle school (MS). A few teachers read, summarised and presented activities for the rest of the MS teachers from some key chapters in *Schools That Learn*. We spent that whole day in the school library together and from the start the engagement of the teachers told me this was going to be significant. By going through some of Senge's exercises designed to help us surface our underlying assumptions about education, we began to engage in a level of dialogue that I had not previously witnessed in a school.

We started by looking at the purposes of schooling and how we ended up with the system we have inherited. In *Schools That Learn* (2000: 35–48), Senge and colleagues have compiled a list of underlying 'assumptions' that appear to be implicit in our 'industrial age' approach to education when viewed from a systems thinking perspective (i.e. seeing the overall effect, not just the intended outcomes). We focused on seven of these.

SEVEN ASSUMPTIONS ABOUT EDUCATION

1. Children are deficient and schools fix them.

2. Learning takes place in the head, not in the body as a whole.

3. Everyone learns, or should learn, in the same way.

4. Learning takes place in the classroom, not in the world.

5. Knowledge is inherently fragmented.

6. Schools communicate 'The Truth'.

7. Learning is primarily individualistic and competition accelerates learning.

When seen in the light of systems thinking these implicit assumptions about schooling emerge, and we can understand better perhaps how those physical and emotional taxonomies developed by Bloom (see Chapter 1) came to disappear from view.

After exploring this together we asked 'What hidden assumptions might underlie our own beliefs about how children learn best?'

We openly considered the impact our own schooling might have had on our seldom-examined views about the nature of human learning and modern schooling. This approach called on something personal in our teachers and created a secure, shared

(Continued)

(Continued)

foundation for communal reflection and exploration. Many of the comments from teachers in their feedback on the professional development (PD) day reflected this deeper level of engagement:

> 'I loved it. I thought a time to slow down, pause, reflect and think collectively was the greatest thing.'

> 'I found it to be really productive. We rarely have time to really talk to colleagues. I gained some new perspectives and working with others helped me to sort out what I thought/believed.'

> 'I like time to think theoretically/idealistically. It helps to push our conceptual thinking about schools.'

> 'I liked this PD day a lot. I think it was very effective, offering lots of new stuff/ discussing known things from a new angle/in depth.'

> 'I thought the day was productive, as I think that we seldom get the opportunity to use PD time to really engage each other. Typically we are absorbing ideas from outside sources and experts. These sessions have value as well, of course, but too often we neglect what we have to offer each other.'

> 'By far one of the best MS PD's ever. Quality use of time, thought provoking discussions and the subject matter was relevant and is ongoing.'

The outcome from this single day was a set of common agreements about 'What really matters in middle school'. As we began to put together our ideas about what, in an ideal world, we would want a middle school education to look like, we began to discover a lot of commonality. With hindsight this may seem quite obvious, but at the time it was very important that we, as a group of 30 educators about to embark on a journey of change, could visualise and explicitly articulate the common ground we had to work from – and to.

At the same time the whole school (i.e. elementary, middle and upper) was going through a mission review and whilst I believe ISP did genuinely seek to live its mission, I felt that reaching these common agreements in the middle school was of far greater significance to the way learning was to unfold and evolve over the next few years than anything else we had tried. It wasn't that we set out on a well-defined 'three-year strategic plan' or had clear outcomes and assessment in place to indicate progress towards meeting targets. Sometimes such approaches can work quite well, but often schools get lost in the details and fail to really meet their objectives on a more fundamental level. I think it was much simpler than that – we had created a touchstone, a set of signposts to check in with from time to time and, when necessary, amend. Importantly, thanks to the personal reflection and dialogue processes, we had reached a level of common agreement that each teacher could subscribe to from the heart. In the final part of the session we used questions to engage teachers which contained key phrases from the school's mission statement:

'What is your personal vision of the educational experiences that can "promote a healthy, fulfilling and purposeful life"?'

'How do you best "engage, inspire and empower" your students?'

'What excites you about the possibilities of further developments?'

'What limiting factors do you perceive?'

The surprising thing to me was that, even without doing a lot of detailed planning, when we looked back a few years later, we had made really significant progress towards some of those key items. Others we had not done so well on, so we then had to decide whether to consciously plan to work towards those ends – or to let them go.

In this way, our ideas about 'what really matters' seeped into the psyche of our school and over time some quite transformational ideals were actualised. I believe that on an almost subliminal level the deep dialogue and those big picture objectives were continually impacting our choices about where to put our precious time and energy – about what to include and, crucially, what to let go of or to refuse to take on. As schools and as teachers we often take on too much, so it's important to look at this directly and to support each other in not trying do everything that appears to be necessary – to simplify and to give ourselves permission to say 'no' or 'not now'.

Understanding the overall impact of the system within which we operate as educators is fundamental to helping to change that system, to help it become more humane. Despite our best intentions for our learners, schooling often ends up giving messages to students that may not be wholly beneficial. A young person could be forgiven for thinking that education is all about getting the grade so that you can book your place in university, so that you can get the job you most want and deserve, so that you can earn the money you need to buy the house for the family that you want. That you work hard so you can finally retire and relax. That life is a journey from A to B, to C to D, and that at some point in the future we can end up someplace where we will be happy and successful. But learning is about life, not just preparation for college.

THE OVERLAP OF PROFESSIONAL DEVELOPMENT AND PERSONAL GROWTH

In some of the examples we saw in Chapter 6 of schools that have made progress in implementing a more holistic vision, there was an important element of choice for teachers in terms of how they wanted to personally engage with the trainings being offered. Although mindfulness is highly adaptable and (I believe) potentially beneficial for all, I do not think that teachers should be forced to take mindful awareness courses. However, if a school decides to focus on wellbeing, then it does become incumbent on all teachers to be involved in some way or other. For me this is a bit like what happened when IT hit a certain stage in its development in education. For a while it was only the early enthusiasts who engaged with computers, ran networks, led the way in the classroom. But at a certain point in most schools it became untenable for a teacher to say 'I don't use computers in my classroom'. After a while there was no negotiation – it just became 'this is what we do here'. And I believe that the same could happen with a shift towards wellbeing becoming an overarching construct for a variety of life-enhancing approaches in schools.

Not everyone wants to learn to meditate, but it would be good to at least give all teachers a grounded, experiential introduction to mindfulness so they know first-hand what it's about, rather than having an opinion based on an indirect understanding. In my experience of working with schools where some teachers might seem initially resistant, once they have received a proper introduction most will say 'Oh, I get it now, *that's* what it's about'. They may not want to train in or teach mindfulness themselves, but if the school does decide to develop this area they are less likely to undermine the initiative if they have a direct understanding of it. A few may well continue to be sceptical, but many will also feel that this is very important for themselves as well as for students.

If we situate mindfulness awareness training under a holistic umbrella of wellbeing, flourishing, or whatever concept works best for a particular school community, then we can give teachers different options to choose from for their own growth and development within that framework. In this way, we establish a culture in which enhancing wellbeing in our school community is something we can all subscribe to in some form or other – a 'highest common denominator'.

Social neuroscience provides education with ample support for the notion that, because teaching is such a social profession, and because the role of the teacher depends upon evolutionary predispositions that speak to the core of human learning through relationship, it is simply not enough to say 'I teach History [or Geography, or Math] and that's that'. Deep and effective learning for our students is so dependent on a range of teacher skills and capacities, as well as on the teacher's embodied presence, that developing these capacities in ourselves, as best we can, needs to become just a normal part of the job. For many of us the chance to engage in areas of professional development that overlap with our personal growth is simply a bonus. If nothing else because it can make the difference between an enjoyable, sustainable career and one that may lead to exhaustion or burnout.

If time and space is eventually found for genuine dialogue within a whole school community on the topic of wellbeing, and if the school then decides to shift the focus in this area, there is still no need to rush towards implementation. If a change of attitude has occurred this in itself can inform curriculum planning and adoption of new initiatives. Looking through the integrative lens of mindfulness-based wellbeing, a school can begin to see many opportunities to build in a range of strategies that can result in a much healthier community.

THE MINDFUL SCHOOL LEADER

Cultivating mindful awareness in our leadership and administrative work has rich potential for, us and I will come back to this point at the end of this section. First though, I want to focus on suggestions for supporting school leaders who aim to introduce mindfulness into their school community. If you already have experience in mindfulness or meditation yourself, this puts you in an excellent position to begin to work with others in your school. It is such a powerful model to see heads of school and directors working from this kind of background. Rare, but it does exist! If you don't have this experience, no problem, all you really need to get started is interest and enthusiasm.

Suggestions for school leaders:

- Identify any teachers, administrators, parents, board members or governors who are meditation practitioners and who might be capable of leading voluntary sessions for interested teachers and parents.

- If you can help develop a group of teachers who are interested in mindfulness, then seek out local adult mindfulness trainers to provide them with an 8-week course.

- If you already have some teachers with a background in mindfulness in education in your school, these are the people to ally with. Let them know of your interest in supporting them. This may just be moral support to begin with but hopefully at some point it will become more practical, for example providing funding for further training, setting aside time at staff meetings and so on.

- The most common pathway we see in schools is where an interest in mindfulness starts with one or two enthusiastic teachers (or counsellors or educational psychologists). They are self-motivated and may have already done a mindfulness course for themselves. Sometimes they may have already gone on to get themselves trained to teach mindfulness to students. By showing your support here you give a strong message to everyone that you and the school care about teacher health and sustainability.

- Consider asking a leading teacher with mindfulness experience to present to staff or bring in a specialist to introduce mindfulness and wellbeing. *See this as the start of a dialogue rather than the implementation of an action plan.*

- If you are in a school fortunate enough to have educational psychologists, school counsellors or pastoral/wellbeing specialists on the faculty, you can engage them in this work. They are well placed, as professionals responsible for 'the heart of the school' both in terms of expertise and organisational processes, to help facilitate, and sometimes supervise, initiatives that holistically promote mindfulness, affective skills and wellbeing.

- Once you have a few key people who have completed the adult training, see if you can continue to support them by finding time for them to meet together, within professional development time if possible. Through sharing experiences they will build community and support each other to allow their growing mindful awareness to impact their teaching (i.e., teaching mindfully).

- If you take some training yourself, this makes such a strong statement to the school community – and it will probably also benefit you directly!

- Once the foundations are in place, look for good-quality courses to get some teachers with an established personal practice trained up to teach mindfulness to students (see page 108).

- Don't rush this process, let it grow organically – and don't expect teachers who are certified to teach mindfulness to start to train their colleagues. If other teachers are interested, encourage them to take adult mindfulness courses for themselves as the essential first step. This is so important as otherwise teachers may rush into teaching students without the necessary expertise or experience. Although mindfulness teaching looks very simple, it's also easy to turn people off it if not done with integrity.

- Consider developing a plan for ongoing training of staff with various entry levels. For an example of this, see *The American School of the Hague Continuum* at the end of the chapter.

- Consider focusing a staff training course on wellbeing, perhaps along the lines of the Schools That Learn exercise, to help examine assumptions about *what really matters* in learning.

- Consider initiating a dialogue with the school community, including parents, teachers and students in discussions around wellbeing.

- Look at your curriculum development plan to see where mindfulness training for students could best be located, for example as part of PSHE, in advisory or tutorial groups, as stand-alone classes, or initially as optional courses.

- Consider the best year group for your school to start training students and how to spiral development of mindful awareness experiences.

- When you are looking at whole-school development planning, consider how best to embed this area into the school's future. *Is it time for a health and wellbeing review?*

- Consider evolving an holistic, long-term plan of *how* and *where* mindfulness training can best be woven in with affective skills/SEL and existing courses and activities. *See the 'Flourishing' framework in Chapter 6, for an example of coherent mapping of the skills and experiences students will encounter as they progress through the school.*

- Consider connecting with a local university who might be interested in doing some research on mindfulness in schools. There are many researchers wanting to work on this these days.

- Connect with other Heads and schools on a similar path. As you take these initial steps, mutual support and learning from each other is extremely helpful.

- Build community in your school around this. *It will pay off – you will have more sensitive, less reactive teachers; better student–teacher relations; students with a practical, life-skills toolkit; and a saner, perhaps even happier, school environment. You are shifting the focus!*

Figure 7.1 at the end of this chapter offers a simplified version of possible approaches to introducing mindfulness in schools.

ADVICE FROM EDUCATORS

'You have to allow it time to become embedded. This journey started for us when we offered it to staff and it was only a year later that staff got to go on the training courses to teach it to students. Over time what really makes a difference is the students and what they say about it. It's powerful for teachers to hear that student voice.'

Primary School Head

'Go slow. It's better to be authentic than push something through that feels forced.'

Secondary School Teacher

'Take it slowly! A few key adults who are invested in their own practice will be able to generate interest and excitement. Practice! Without your own genuine practice, this won't work.'

Secondary School Counsellor

There is a potential contradiction to be aware of that leaders supporting mindfulness for teachers may face at some point: some teachers may complain that 'School tells me they want me to teach mindfulness and be more mindful but at the same time they are giving me too much to do and causing me stress'. I feel that this is a contradiction, not an hypocrisy, and we are dealing here with the realities of school life. We do, however, need to be able to openly discuss:

- taking better care of ourselves;
- finding ways of reducing stress on ourselves and on our students wherever possible.

WHAT'S IN IT FOR ME?

In addition to the positive changes a more mindful school brings, as a leader you can personally gain a great deal from developing mindful awareness in your professional and personal life. That's basically what this book is about, so I don't need to recap here the benefits of mindfulness per se. But it is worth noting that quite often administrators and school leaders, even when they appreciate the value of developing these areas for their teachers and students, are often the last to feel they could invest the time and effort for their own benefit. This is probably due mainly to work and time pressures. But the positive benefits we can draw from mindfulness training for ourselves are well worth making the effort for. As an attuned, sensitive leader who knows how to manage their stress effectively and who has the empathic skills and understanding to support others in this area, you can become a powerful role model for teachers and students. And we are very much in need of positive, wise and sympathetic models of leadership – people who can demonstrate a balance of cleverness with wisdom, analytical skills with compassion, head with heart.

ACCEPTANCE

I guess I have always been somebody who was driven by feelings, moods and body sensations. I was never, though, very conscious of my thoughts – I would be more driven by my gut and stomach as a teacher. Working under leaders who caused a lot of stress made me wake up in the morning overcome with a wave of nausea. During my mindfulness training I was tracking through the day to see what was causing it. Someone on the course normalised this for me – not every thought is true and I don't have to be ruled by thoughts or body sensations. So, if I'm feeling really queasy this morning, maybe I've just got a stomach-ache and that's okay. Acceptance rather than rumination. That was amazing for me – I got some perspective and control over my thoughts and my body and that was a massive turning point. I'm someone who wears her heart on her sleeve and the understanding mindfulness brought me has helped me to step back a bit from those emotions. Not that I don't still have them – being empathetic and having good emotional intelligence is important for a leader – but I am not as flaky as I used to be! I certainly wouldn't have been able to take these fast promotions without the ability to ground myself.

School Principal

For myself, aside from giving me a renewed enthusiasm for my work – and especially for the daily connections with children and adults – I found that the development of mindful awareness had many applications in my work as a Principal. I want to share one practical example here that illustrates this overlapping of mindful awareness and social-emotional competencies, of personal growth and professional development.

DIFFICULT CONVERSATIONS

I found that increased self-awareness helped me regulate my emotional responses in challenging situations. Dealing with conflict and difficult interactions can be a challenge for any teacher. Having 'difficult conversations', sometimes with parents but especially with colleagues, is one of the most testing aspects of being an administrator. These are skills worth cultivating in any career or relationship, but surprisingly they seldom feature in teacher or administrator training.

Over my time in Prague I developed an approach that worked really well for me. I drew on the *Crucial Conversations* (Patterson et al., 2002) and *Crucial Confrontations* (Patterson et al., 2005) books and mixed in my own mindful awareness elements. When I had a tricky conversation coming up I would first reflect, either by meditating or journaling or talking it through with a sympathetic colleague. I focused on identifying the predominant feeling underlying my state of mind:

- Was I angry with a teacher for what, I had been informed, was some unjust, mean or petty behaviour on their part? Perhaps something that had caused a student pain or discomfort?

- Or was I feeling guilty because I had been aware of an issue for some time but was only now moving to take action?

- Was it a bit of both? Or something else?

Whatever it was, by naming it, facing it, *owning it* before I sat down with the person, I found I could transform the 'feel', and thus the result, of the targeted conversation.

GETTING ALONGSIDE

I called this 'getting alongside' because what it did for me – and, I felt, also for the teacher – was to remove the sense of interpersonal tension or power-struggle that might have got in the way of dealing with the issue itself. It enabled me to present the problem in a way that the teacher could engage with. Getting the issue out and clearly on the table so we could sit alongside each other (figuratively, but sometimes literally) and work out how to approach the problem, instead of putting them on the defensive. The emphasis would still be on the teacher to deal with the issue and it seemed to empower them to grasp the nettle and to go away with a clearer understanding as well as the resolve to deal with it.

Sometimes taking these reflective moments and using observation to clarify what was going on internally could open up valuable space for me. Just giving myself permission to *not* have to solve this problem now and to not let my role as a figure of authority put undue pressure on me, was enough to loosen the tension. Recognising that the solution needed to rest with the other person in this case could also help transform the way I was inwardly approaching the situation. Acknowledging these feelings of anger, guilt, confusion and pressure doesn't necessarily mean they will go away, but it does mean we can work *with* them and not let them muddy the waters. Keeping a clear head amidst turbulence and turmoil is something school leaders prize highly, and mindfulness can certainly support this.

WHAT ABOUT THE PARENTS?

This question inevitably comes up in relation to introducing mindful awareness programmes to schools. Of course it depends very much on your particular school community setting, but in my experience this has not been a problem for parents. In fact, quite the opposite - sometimes parents are very much wanting something like this, and it's the school that might prove to be more resistant.

In the case of the International School of Prague (ISP), at the time (2008) I was starting to teach mindfulness it was all very new - unheard of even - and seeing as I was the Principal anyway I just started doing it and didn't tell the parents. I was, though, always expecting to get a tap on the shoulder at a parent conference and to be challenged about doing something so unusual, especially if parents assumed that it was some kind of religious indoctrination. I had had no complaints - or questions even - but then, in the third year, at a middle school (11–14 years) parent conference, just as I had imagined, a parent came up to me, tapped me on the shoulder and said, 'Mr Hawkins, about this "mindfulness" thing you're teaching,' and I thought, 'Here we go - finally!'

'Well,' she continued, 'I was driving my son to school last week and we were late, stuck in traffic and I hate being stuck in traffic and I hate being late so I was going on about the traffic and then he interrupted me and said "Hey mum, it's okay. Don't worry. Try this: just try and notice your hands on the steering wheel; just relax your fingers a little ..." which I did and then he took me through this breathing exercise and it really helped and so I said "Where are you getting this from?" and he said "Mr Hawkins" and he started to talk about all these things I had no idea he knew about. So anyway, Mr Hawkins, I just wanted to say thank you for teaching him this stuff - he said it really helps - especially in sports.'

Perhaps not all parents would see it that way, but the truth is many parents are stressed too and often interested in something that they think might help them - and their children - to learn to relax and to focus. I did then start to tell parents about the courses, and about a year later some members of the School Community Association asked me to speak about mindful awareness training at a middle school coffee morning. We often offered sessions on school developments at these monthly meetings, so I said 'Sure, why not?'. They put up some posters about it and, whereas an average middle school coffee morning might draw about 30-40 parents to these 8.15 a.m. sessions, on this particular day the room was packed - over 60 parents.

Towards the end of the session someone asked if they could organise a sign-up to see if anyone wanted further training for themselves. I said sure, but was totally surprised by the size of the scrum in the corner of the room at the end - the sign-up sheet soon became three sheets as 45 middle school parents put them-selves down for an 8-week evening course!

Emma Naisbett from English Martyr's school in Liverpool, UK has had a similar experience to mine.

'Parents have noticed it too. They've been coming in saying 'My child has been doing this ...' or 'He's been telling me to do this exercise'. If parents are having an argument children are sometimes suggesting that they need to do this or that practice. One parent sent a photograph in, she had walked in on her child and she was doing a practice together with a friend on FaceTime. Other parents told me that one girl was in a community sports team competition and she taught the entire team a breathing practice because they were all very nervous. So the whole team, whether they went to our school or not, was doing the breathing exercise she led.'

With a 90 per cent Muslim population, I was curious to know if there had been any parental opposition to compulsory mindfulness training for 7 to 10-year-olds at Amy Footman's Stanley Grove primary school in Manchester:

'None. I think it comes down to the really good relationship we have with the community. We wrote them an excited letter about it. We feel they trust that we want to do what's best for their children.'

Some schools inform parents about mindfulness programmes from the beginning, but some choose not to, as is the case with many curriculum initiatives. Depending on your context, offering a parent information evening can be a good idea, especially if it is framed within the context of a dialogue about wellbeing. It may be the exception, but in some schools the initial motivation for mindfulness training has actually come from the parent community. Of course these days mindfulness is very much in the public consciousness, thanks to a lot of media attention, so many parents already know something about it, and in fact quite a few may have come across it through friends or family or through its use in the workplace. A number of large multinational companies (such as Google, General Mills and Apple), many universities and hospitals (including the Mayo Clinic), as well as a number of services, such as police forces, army and US Marines, now include mindfulness in their staff training programmes.

In the final chapter we consider how we can align our efforts in developing mindful awareness and affective skills training in schools with this growing appreciation of the value of these skills in the wider world.

WHAT REALLY MATTERS?

- Going slowly.
- Creating safe space for deeper dialogue.
- Open-minded, supportive school leadership.
- Persistence.

Raise Awareness *Start a dialogue*	• Introductions to mindfulness and social and emotional learning for staff, students and leadership *(internally from teachers, or externally from outside specialists)* • Parent community (or parent and teacher community) workshops

Train and Practice
 	
Be mindful
Teach mindfully
Teach mindfulness
	BE MINDFUL
	
	Options for initial training:
	• Locate a local adult trainer (8-week group courses)
	   ○ *Mindfulness-Based Stress Reduction (MBSR)*
	   ○ *Mindfulness-Based Cognitive Therapy (MBCT)*
	   ○ *Mindfulness in Schools Project '.b Foundations' (UK)*
	   ○ *Breathworks Mindfulness Courses (UK)*
	
	• Take an online course
	   ○ *University of Massachusetts Medical School Centre for Mindfulness (MBSR)*
	
	• Follow a self-directed course
	   ○ *'Mindfulness', an 8-week course, 'Finding Peace in a Frantic World'*
	
	Practising:
	• Formal and informal practices
	• Mindfulness meditation apps
	• Mindfulness meditation retreats

	TEACH MINDFULLY • Cultivating Awareness and Resilience in Education (CARE) course • Stress Management and Resiliency Techniques (SMART) course • Not many other courses available as yet, but some helpful books in *Further Reading* Chapters 4 and 5
	TEACH MINDFULNESS • *Mindfulness in Schools Project '.b' (11–18 yrs) Paws b (7–11 yrs)* • *MBSR-T – Stressed Teens Programme (online)* • *Still Quiet Place (5–18) (online)* • *Mindful Schools (5–18) (online and onsite)*
Embed and Extend *Whole-school culture*	• School support for teachers in both classroom and personal practice • Co-ordination and supervision of mindfulness teaching • Identify staff needs on a training needs continuum (see page 159) • Spiralling mindful awareness curriculum • Connecting to larger framework of wellbeing and social and emotional learning • Making connections to other subject areas and school activities • Mission/vision – integrated academic + social-emotional planning

Figure 7.1 Pathways to mindfulness-based wellbeing for school communities

Note: Only a few examples are listed here for each stage.

A MINDFULNESS PROFESSIONAL DEVELOPMENT CONTINUUM

Created by Bart Dankaerts and Kili Lay

American School of The Hague

You can use this continuum to assess where you are and how to get to the next level. If you are interested in getting some mindfulness training, please discuss your interest with your divisional principal.

Being Mindful

Step 1: Curious newcomer

- WHO: for people who have no prior experience with mindfulness and are curious to find out more about what it is and how they might use it in their own life.

- WHAT: an 8-week course (about 1-hour meeting time per week) based on the '.b' course that is also taught to students. Apart from the 1-hour a week meeting time, participants would also be expected to spend about 5-15 minutes per day practising some techniques at home.

Step 2: Beginner

- WHO: for people who have completed the 'curious newcomer' course or have some prior experience with mindfulness who want to further develop their own personal mindfulness practice.

- WHAT: a year-long subscription to Headspace (www.headspace.com/) that allows individuals to develop their own personal practice. This would require about 20-30 minutes of practice every day.

Step 3: Curious practitioner

- WHO: for people who have established a personal mindfulness practice routine and want to deepen their own personal practice in view of getting licensed to teach mindfulness to students.

- WHAT: an 8-week MBSR course (about 2-hours meeting time per week plus personal practice at home). This course can be taught at ASH if we have enough people signing up.

Teaching Mindfully

Step 4: The mindful teacher

- WHO: for teachers with their own personal mindfulness practice routine who want to develop strategies and practices for implementing mindfulness into their daily teaching routines.
- WHAT: a 1-day Teaching Mindfully workshop with MindWell.

Teaching Mindfulness

Step 5: Experienced practitioner

- WHO: for people who want to teach mindfulness to students. In order to qualify for this course, the MBSR course (described in the 'Curious practitioner' level) is a prerequisite.
- WHAT: a 4-day '.b' (for 11 to 18-year-olds) or Paws b (for 7 to 11-year-olds) certification course (http://mindfulnessinschools.org/). This course is taught several times a year at various locations around Europe and the rest of the world. With sufficient interest, it can also be organised locally at ASH.

TRY IT OUT!

For yourself:

- Formal practice – try:
  - extending your formal sitting time
  - exploring mindful walking (see page 47)
  - or doing a longer bodyscan (page 47).
- Informal practice:
  - Try some of the ideas for *Weaving It In* on page 49 to keep bringing you back to the body and being more the present in school this week:
    - journal your observations
    - be gentle with yourself when you fail to remember to use them
    - renew your intention to try again.
- Consider taking a local MBSR, MBCT or similar adult mindfulness course.

- o If there are none available locally, check out online or self-guided courses (see Figure 7.1).
- o Consider going on a mindfulness meditation retreat.

For your school:

- **Consider using some of the approaches and exercises** from *Schools That Learn* by Peter Senge as outlined on pages 146–149. Depending on the needs of your school, you could start by surfacing assumptions about schooling in general or about the importance of wellbeing, mindfulness, SEL and affective skills.

- **School Leaders** (and Trailblazers!): Check out the suggestions on page 151–152. Using the Pathways framework (Figure 7.1), take time to reflect on what could be an entry point for your school. Who can help you discuss ideas on getting started?

If you already have an established mindful meditation practice, consider:

- Starting a short practice session for teachers and staff before or after school (or at lunch time).

- Setting up a drop in session for students or an after school activity to introduce interested students to secular mindful meditation.

- Training to become a teacher of mindfulness!

FURTHER READING AND RESOURCES

Senge, P., Cambron-McCabe, N. Lucas, T., Smith, B., Dutton, J. and Kleiner, A. (2000) *Schools That Learn: A Fifth Discipline Fieldbook for Educators, Parents, and Everyone Who Cares About Education*. London: Nicholas Brealey.

Senge and his team unlock the underlying and outmoded assumptions that hold education systems together and explore communal ways to make deep, systemic change.

Marturano, J. (2014) *Finding the Space to Lead: A Practical Guide to Mindful Leadership*. New York: Bloomsbury.

There are many mindful leadership coaches out there, but Marturano's work seems to resonate especially well with school leaders.

Abbott, J. and MacTaggart, H. (2010) *Overschooled but Undereducated: How the Crisis in Education is Jeopardizing our Adolescents*. London: 21st Century Learning Initiative.

Some radical thinking about schooling and how it goes 'against the grain of the adolescent brain'.

Goleman, D. and Senge, P. (2014) *Triple Focus: A New Approach to Education* (Kindle edn). Florence, MA: More than Sound.

A very quick read, but a thought-provoking rationale for reframing schooling.

Powell, W. and Kusuma-Powell, O. (2013) The OIQ Factor: Raising Your School's Organizational Intelligence. Woodbridge: John Catt Educational.

An intelligent and practical resource written by wise, experienced educators:

'Teachers and school leaders must step back from the day-today focus of getting more done, of striving after 'results' and carve out sacred time for personal and group development... Raising organizational intelligence is all about re-culturing schools...It requires a change not just in behaviors and skills, but in values, beliefs and even identity.'

8

Beyond Our Classrooms: Aligning with the Wider World

This chapter:

⤳ looks at current developments (local and global) that can help give individuals, schools and educational organisations a sense of alignment and empowerment

⤳ takes heart from some interesting initiatives in universities to ask if it is time for a 'new metric' that targets and measures wellbeing alongside academic achievement in schools and colleges

⤳ considers the value of a more balanced education for individuals, society and the planet.

Focusing on *what really matters* can help us keep our sights set on the deeper purposes of education. When we look beyond the walls of our own classroom or school, we find a range of developments - in education and beyond - that echo an understanding of the value of shifting our focus to include affective areas of human experience more centrally in learning. We can strengthen the reach and the relevance of work in mindful awareness training, and in social-emotional learning, if we take a broader view - considering the context and seeing the bigger picture through aligning our efforts with what is already happening elsewhere in education and in the wider world.

When we pose the question 'What do we really want for our children and for our society?' it can lead us to a deeper dialogue about the purpose of government. If economic growth is not an end in itself, what is the end? Is there a higher goal that encompasses creating a healthy, sustainable society? Some governments have begun to revisit this question and there has been significant interest in the economics of wellbeing. What you measure is important; it affects how you plan and therefore what you get, and by measuring progress towards wellbeing as well as GDP, we are in a better position to support movement in this direction. Economic prosperity is not necessarily making us happier, beyond having what is necessary for security and comfort. If we can begin to understand more about how to train and educate ourselves for a wiser, more compassionate and sustainable society, then the part that schools play in preparing our young people for this will become highly significant.

POSITIVE PSYCHOLOGY

Some schools, especially in Australia, but also increasingly in many (mainly independent) schools in the UK, have developed approaches to learning based on positive psychology (see for example, Wellington College Happiness and Wellbeing approach at www.wellingtoncollege.org.uk/2288/school-life/well-being/). The work of Martin Seligman, a leading authority of positive psychology, has stimulated interest in businesses and institutions to find ways to increase our ability to 'flourish'. This focus on our wellbeing, rather than on what makes us unwell, has had a powerful impact in many areas of science and society.

There is some serious economic and sociological research behind this recent focus on how to measure and promote a flourishing society. Felicia Huppert, founder and former Director of the Well-being Institute at the University of Cambridge, was involved in a major European study (the European Social Survey) to measure and compare various elements of just what it is that makes for a healthy nation. Methods have been developed to quantify resilience, relationship, engagement, self-esteem and so on, for example, and then to be able to compare these characteristics across different countries.

Developing happiness and wellbeing indicators as a way to measure and guide public policy is certainly an area that global institutions such as the OECD, UNICEF and the UN now support. In 2011, an initiative from Bhutan has resulted in happiness becoming an official UN indicator of national development (Helliwell et al., 2015).

DEVELOPMENTS IN MINDFULNESS IN EDUCATION

So if some nations, global communities and global organisations are beginning to recognise the importance of conscious and strategic planning to promote wellbeing, are educational organisations also beginning to recognise this?

Although only small steps have been taken, we are beginning to see some significant developments. Working with educators around the world, we see that in recent years some schools and organisations are moving to shift the focus in this direction. Mindfulness in education tends to follow on from developments in mental health, and often a well-established use of mindfulness in mental health in a country puts adult mindfulness practitioners in a good position to help spread those skills to teachers once the interest in mindfulness in education begins to stir.

United Kingdom

On a national level, the UK is a leading example of development in mindfulness in education. There is perhaps a greater understanding of mindfulness at senior levels of government in the UK than in most other countries in the world at this moment. Jon Kabat-Zinn visited Downing Street in 2012, and in 2013 Thich Nhat Hanh led a meditation in the House of Lords. Since then Mark Williams introduced mindfulness to Westminster, and together with Chris Cullen and Richard Burnett they have trained MPs and peers on 8-week mindfulness courses that have become quite popular. Some politicians have spoken out in public about the effect this has had on them:

> Lord Andrew Stone spoke of how mindfulness had helped him face the stress of difficult negotiations during a recent trip to Egypt, while the Conservative MP Tracey Crouch shared how mindfulness has helped her emerge from a place of anxiety that led her to take antidepressants, and about which she's only just felt able to go public. (Halliwell, 2014)

> 'I am one of about 130 MPs and peers who have taken a mindfulness course in Parliament in the past three and a half years. Like many of my colleagues, I found the course compelling, with personal benefits for everyday life.

> Abundant research shows that attention is fundamental to mental functioning. The eight-week mindfulness course undertaken by parliamentarians taught us how to train our attention to remain more focused and engaged in the experience of the present moment. By steadying one's attention in that way, one can learn to respond in more clear-headed, versatile and creative ways to daily choices and challenges, instead of being driven by habit and impulse. Those simple, accessible mental skills can be taught to everyone, but, as with so many things, the most effective time to learn is during childhood'. (Nicholas Dakin, MP, September 2016)

In 2015 Mindfulness All-Party Parliamentary Group reported to the British parliament on its year of researching the power and potential of mindfulness training in prisons, mental health and education (see Chapter 5).

Over the last few years there has been considerable growth in schools throughout the UK (including many state schools) that are beginning to train up teachers and students in mindful awareness.

Other Countries

Developments in mindfulness in education are taking place all around the world, and here are just a few examples to illustrate this:

- In the USA there are multiple approaches to using mindfulness in numerous contexts. In his book *A Mindful Nation* (2012), Congressmen Tim Ryan outlined various ways in which mindfulness can contribute to modern society. He received a $1m federal grant to teach mindfulness in schools in his home district of Ohio.

- In Canada there are various initiatives underway, notably in British Columbia where they have been tracking children's wellbeing and introducing social-emotional learning programmes, some now mindfulness based, for many years.

- In Europe, Germany, and in particular The Netherlands, have well-developed approaches to establishing mindfulness in education.

- In Australia there is a background in positive psychology in a number of schools, and some are now beginning to combine this with mindfulness.

- In New Zealand the Mental Health Foundation provides mindfulness courses for schools that support the Ministry of Education's unique concept of *Hauora* wellbeing for all.

- In Asia there are, of course, many countries where meditation is part of the religion and culture. In Singapore, the prioritisation of social and emotional skills mentioned in Chapter 6 potentially provides a new context for mindful awareness training in schools, and even some Buddhist organisations are now sending counsellors and psychologists for training in Western, secular versions of mindfulness for schools.

The following is an example of efforts underway to bring such training to the University of Hong Kong.

HONG KONG UNIVERSITY, PSYCHOLOGY DEPARTMENT

Modern approaches to training adults in secular mindfulness in Hong Kong have primarily been introduced through Dr Helen Ma in association with the Oxford Mindfulness Centre. The Department of Psychology at the University of Hong Kong is now preparing the ground to teach mindfulness to educational psychologists, teachers and students.

Professor Shui-fong Lam, Director of the Educational Psychology Programme, HKU, states:

My intention at HKU Psychology Department is to embed MBCT [Mindfulness Based Cognitive Therapy] in undergraduate courses in a 12-week term. Because they are psychology students I hope that they can have an experiential learning of MBCT on top of the theoretical understanding of cognitive therapy and mindfulness.

I became interested in mindfulness through a student I supervised for his PhD thesis. I was not an expert but I was interested because I know the validities and method of research and I know a little about mindfulness. His research compared 14–15-year-old students after mindfulness and loving kindness training with a control group. Because I was involved I really witnessed how mindfulness made an impact on the children. Hard data and evidence showed that it helps those with stress problems but those without stress can also use it to flourish and thrive. Seeing how it worked with the young adolescents made me feel that I should really put it forward.

There is a huge need for mindfulness but because it is so competitive here people feel there is no time to fit it in. Hong Kong is especially competitive in the educational system. It is like a pressure cooker. We are in an examination-oriented culture and we put all the emphasis on academics, not on social and emotional learning. There is a scramble for places in college so students have lots of stress. We have the unfortunate 'record' for the youngest suicide in the world for educational reasons: recently, a 7-year-old child took his own life after doing badly on a Chinese dictation test.

I have taught mindfulness to students who could not survive in the mainstream schools. These are the underdogs. At first they were very indifferent but some of them became more attentive. I saw that even the most naughty and uncooperative kids felt some interest in this because of their experiences of tension, stress and low self-esteem. The 8-week experience was somehow very different from their other courses. I feel happy that they liked it. It opened a little door so they can remember it in the future.

INTERNATIONAL EDUCATION

- The European Council for International Schools has for some time had a conference strand dedicated to health and nutrition, but since 2014 they also have a committee that focuses specifically on promoting 'Flourishing in Schools'.

- The Council of International Schools accrediting inspections of international schools now includes student and whole-school community wellbeing in their standards.

- The International Baccalaureate Organization has recently started to promote both mindfulness and affective skills in their revised approaches to learning.

- The International School Counselor Association has recently highlighted mindfulness training for counsellors.

Pie in the Sky?

As educators trying to make schools more responsive to the full range of needs of our students we often get frustrated by the slow pace of change and invariably it seems that the demands of tertiary education preclude deep change in our schools. Our confusion about whether the real goal of secondary education is preparation for life and work or a filtering system for college has significant knock-on effects. So, can we really put student welfare at the top of our agendas? Or does all this sound too idealistic – too 'pie in the sky'?

Perhaps it does, but things *do* change – even tertiary education systems.

UNIVERSITY AND COLLEGE ADMISSION SYSTEMS – 'TURNING THE TIDE'?

Perhaps one of the biggest obstacles to fundamental change in schools comes from the admissions requirements and processes of universities and colleges. We end up putting so much pressure on young people, and on the schools that work so hard to equip them for increasingly competitive requirements at university entry level and for a rapidly changing job market.

Even here though there are small signs of change in the air. In 2015 George Washington University dropped testing requirements for admissions, joining over 125 private colleges and universities in the USA that now look at more holistic options for determining admissions (Anderson, 2015).

A recent report, 'Harvard turning the tide' (2015), initiated by Harvard Graduate School of Education and supported by over 100 presidents and deans of admission at some of the top colleges throughout the USA, seeks to change the messages communicated to high-school students through the admission process. The report is primarily responding to research showing how young people are becoming less caring (Harvard Graduate School, 2014), but it also recommends less emphasis on standardised test scores. The report recognises that the heavy load of Advance Placement entry exams for college 'is often cited as a culprit in sleep deprivation, anxiety and depression among students at richer schools' (Bruni, 2016). Stephen Farmer, vice provost for enrolment and undergraduate admissions at the University of North Carolina at Chapel Hill, says, 'Just making people jump through hoops because we can – we don't want to do that, especially when some hoops are so arbitrary' (Bruni, 2016).

FILTERING SYSTEMS

Universities and colleges need to take a good look at how their entry standards are negatively affecting students and schooling, and examination boards also need to take more responsibility here. High levels of stress amongst students taking SATs, GCSEs and A Levels in the UK are a rising concern (Stone, 2015). The International Baccalaureate Diploma Programme has recently started to focus on this area with an *IB workload and stress survey*. This 2-year study will assess the impact of the IB diploma programme on students. David Hawley, the IBO's Chief Academic Officer, recognises that some students experience a tremendous amount of stress at this stage of their educational journey and acknowledges that 'we assess the cognitive attributes well ... But we don't give enough attention to social, emotional, wellbeing and health aspects such as "caring","open-minded", "balanced". We want to alert schools about all the developments related to social and emotional learning (SEL) and find ways to provide teacher resources in this area, including what is working in approaches to mindfulness, attention and time management' (Hawley, 2016). (Teachers in IB schools can now access resources to support the development of SEL and mindfulness in the IB's Online Curriculum Centre/Programme Resource Centre.)

If universities do begin to change, this would provide a stimulus for schools to go further in reducing stress and enhancing life skills for wellbeing. Meanwhile, primary (5-10 years) and middle-level (11-14 years) education must hold firm to developmentally appropriate learning that isn't driven too much by pressures from further along the system. As John Dewey said back in 1897,

> Education is not preparation for life; education is life itself. Education, therefore, is a process of living and not a preparation for future living.

So we can't justify teaching something at one stage just because it might be needed at another. The focus has to be on what is relevant and meaningful and necessary for the learner, *now*.

If we can reduce this pressure we will start to make schooling less stressful for students (and teachers) and we can then begin to look more honestly, openly and creatively at *what really matters* – starting from the perspective of the learner rather than simply from the perceived needs of society.

WELLBEING AT UNIVERSITIES – A NEW METRIC?

Many colleges and universities around the world are establishing mindful awareness and wellbeing programmes, partly out of an interest in the potential benefits of mindfulness training but also out of a concern about increasingly disturbing levels of mental health of students.

Here are some examples of recent developments in tertiary education:

- At the University of Montréal, Canada, it is now mandatory if you want to train to be a doctor that you take wellbeing courses that include learning some mindfulness strategies for yourself. Again this is partly because they know that self-care in an extremely demanding profession is increasingly vital and also because of the levels of student stress and distress they are witnessing in medical training.

- The University of Rochester School of Medicine and Dentistry (USA) and Monash Medical School (Australia) have integrated mindfulness into their curricula. At least 12 other medical schools around the world now offer mindfulness training to students. 'Studies show that students who follow these programmes experience decreased psychological distress and an improved quality of life' (Dobkin and Hutchinson, 2013).

- Many universities now offer undergraduate student courses in mindfulness. For example, at Duke University in North Carolina, USA, Koru Mindfulness is an evidence-based curriculum that has been specifically designed for teaching mindfulness, meditation and stress management to college students and other young adults.

- George Mason University in Virginia, USA, is working with faculty and students to focus on wellbeing, drawing on positive psychology and mindfulness. Gallup are carrying out research on the project and Brandon Busteed, Executive Director of Gallup Education, believes that:

> 'Just simply showing that someone has a diploma is not going to be the currency of the future. It's going to be, "Did that diploma significantly increase my likelihood of having a great job and a great life?" *That may be the new metric against which universities are measured in the future.*"' (Watts, 2014).

> You can watch a video about steps being to create a 'wellbeing based university' at George Mason here: https://vimeo.com/114250339

THE HEART OF LEARNING

Leading thinkers around the world have highlighted important areas of learning traditionally overlooked by mainstream educational systems – systems that still focus too much on the sifting of students into convenient batches for further processing after secondary school. Sir Ken Robinson's animated TEDx talk on the outmoded industrial-age approach to education is a good example of this: https://www.ted.com/talks/ken_robinson_changing_education_paradigms

In *Overschooled but Undereducated* (Abbott and MacTaggart, 2010), John Abbott says, 'the world crisis that is upon us is the unintended consequence of an education system designed at another time for another purpose, and now utterly inappropriate to human and planetary needs.' Abbott has dedicated his life to education – to teaching and to synthesising information about our understanding of effective human learning – trying to persuade governments and educational authorities of the urgent need to change our approach to schooling. He is a woodworker as well as an educator, and one of my favourite phrases of his is the metaphor he uses to describe the need for learning that goes with the 'grain of the brain'. As President of the 21st Century Learning Initiative, Abbott is a radical and inspirational thinker and you can find out more about the movement he has inspired, Battling for the Soul of Education, at www.21learn.org.

Peter Senge recently teamed up with the ground-breaking author of *Emotional Intelligence*, Daniel Goleman (1995), to produce a small book entitled '*Triple Focus: A New Approach to Education*' (Goleman and Senge, 2014). In this book the authors argue for three key areas of focus that they believe should form the core of an effective education:

- Focusing inwardly and understanding ourselves.
- Tuning into others and understanding how to form connected relationships.
- Outer-focusing aimed at understanding and integrating with the larger world.

The concept is basically a simple yet powerful combination of *mindfulness*, *SEL* and *systems thinking*. In a complex world, equipping young people with the skills to be able to understand these intricate and overlapping areas is increasingly important. Until very recently, for example, we didn't fully realise the impact that human technological advances are having on the environment – perhaps even on our sustainability as a species. Now that we do know, we have a responsibility and a role to play in both understanding complex systems, such as global warming and climate change, and doing something about it.

Humans are incredibly resourceful. We have such ingenuity and intelligence that if we collectively put our minds to the challenges facing humanity, most problems could be solved or at least made manageable. But we have to set our hearts on it too. It may be no coincidence that we have rising levels of anxiety in our young people at the same time as we have deep, well-publicised fears about our future. Our children are going to need a deep toolbox of inner reserves and competencies to cope with some taxing global issues – environmental, political, religious, psychological – that are not going to go away in a hurry.

Neil Postman, in *The End of Education: Redefining the Value of School* (1995), says 'the narratives that underlie our present conception of school do not serve us well'. Postman describes most educational reforms as 'engineering', concerned with efficiency of delivery, but they 'barely touch the question, What are schools for?'.

We are in need of new narratives that consider the *why* as well as the *how* of education. If I were to start a school from scratch its core focus would be:

> To help our students,
>
> in the context of this community,
>
> learn how best to share this planet.

All key areas of learning – academic, technological, physical and social – can arise from attempting to tackle this central issue. Within this context we can develop foundational skills for building the inner equilibrium and resilience needed to navigate life in the 21st century.

What we often find when we invite teachers and parents to our introductory sessions on mindfulness is a shared sense that something like this is needed, that we are all, to varying degrees, living a little off-centre, and that there is a hunger for a deeper sense of calm and space and for re-connection with our bodies, our emotions and with each other. We see this not just in the privileged private schools of England, not just in the richly resourced international schools of Europe, but also in stretched and stressed inner-city teachers, in schools and organisations in the Americas, Asia and Australasia.

We seem to be increasingly living in isolated pockets. In an age of super-connectivity you might think that we are becoming less isolated. This may be true in some ways, but it only paints part of the picture. We may be more connected 'virtually', but one definition of 'virtually' is 'not quite'. Over the course of the industrial and technological revolutions of the past few centuries, have we lost something along the way? Perhaps a sense of being part of something bigger. Part of a group, a tribe, a people. Of belonging.

The erosion of our traditional communal foundations may go some way to explain why there is currently interest in self-development, emotional awareness and in finding balance. Practices like mindfulness can support efforts to ground ourselves more and to let go of circuitous thinking that can heighten our sense of isolation. In a world where everyone seems overly busy and where no one is really encouraging us to stop for a moment and slow down a little, mindfulness seems to offer a much needed change of pace. Punctuating a busy day with a few moments of calm can bring us back to ourselves. Sharing a silence with others can sometimes be unexpectedly nourishing. A sense of connectedness with a deeper self can bring us closer to others.

It's this same sense of a connected self that might help fill the vacuum experienced by many young people adrift in a world that can feel fragmented, unjust and even psychologically unreal. Unrecognised, this sense of emptiness can leave our young people vulnerable to predatory grooming (sexual, political or religious) and it is the same emptiness that, for many, gets filled through drugs, alcohol or other compulsive or addictive behaviour.

A guiding question for us in this work is, 'Can we, through understanding ourselves and each other better, learn how to cope, thrive and flourish?'

Increased attention skills, deeper self-awareness, better emotional regulation, and improved collaborative skills can all be supported when mindfulness is incorporated into an evolving school culture that weaves 'understanding ourselves' – understanding our minds, our bodies and our emotions – into the core fabric of its work. When combined with a focus on understanding others and understanding our place within the environment and processes in which we live and operate, mindful awareness training can become a valuable component of 21st-century education.

> We aren't teachers.
>
> We are people.
>
> People who teach.

And we're doing the best we can to help young people learn to do the best they can. As teachers, as individuals, there is only so much we can do in the world. But every step we take towards realising our own authenticity and connectedness is a step towards engaging more deeply with ourselves and with our students. Our role, as people who teach, is crucial.

Is mindfulness the answer to all life's problems? I don't believe so. But I do believe that in seeking to validate and support the inner experiences of students and teachers we are asking deep questions – transformative questions – about the way in which we organise schooling, about the sustainability of a teaching career, and about the nourishment of teachers and students. About what really matters in education.

References

Abbott, J. and MacTaggart, H. (2010) *Overschooled but Undereducated: How the Crisis in Education is Jeopardizing our Adolescents*. London: 21st Century Learning Initiative.

Ali, A. (2016) 'Childline expresses concern over rise in number of students under exam stress', *Independent*, 11 May. Available at www.independent.co.uk/student/student-life/health/childline-expresses-concern-over-rise-in-number-of-students-under-exam-stress-a7023746.html (accessed 6/12/16).

Allen, M. (2012) 'Mindfulness and neuroplasticity – a summary of my recent paper', *Neuroconscience*, 23 November. Available at https://neuroconscience.com/2012/11/23/mindfulness_and_plasticity/ (accessed 6/12/16).

American Mindfulness Research Association (2016) 'AMRA resources and services'. Available at https://goamra.org/resources/ (accessed 6/12/16).

Anderson, N. (2015) 'George Washington University applicants no longer need to take admissions tests', *Washington Post*, 27 July. Available at www.washingtonpost.com/news/grade-point/wp/2015/07/27/george-washington-university-applicants-no-longer-need-to-take-admissions-tests/?utm_term=.a9fef78d19f5 (accessed 6/12/16).

Andrews, G., Poulton, R. and Skoog, I. (2005) 'Lifetime risk of depression: restricted to a minority or waiting for most?', *British Journal of Psychiatry*, 187(6): 495–6.

Aspen Institute (2016) 'National Commission of Social, Emotional, and Academic Development'. Available at www.aspeninstitute.org/programs/national-commission-on-social-emotion-al-and-academic-development/ (accessed 6/12/16).

Biegel, G.M., Brown, K.W., Shapiro, S.L. and Schubert, C.M. (2009) 'Mindfulness-based stress reduction for the treatment of adolescent psychiatric outpatients: a randomized clinical trial', *Journal of Consulting and Clinical Psychology*, 77(5): 855–66. Available at www.kirkwarren-brown.vcu.edu/wp-content/pubs/Biegel et al JCCP 2009.pdf (accessed 6/12/16).

Bloom, B., Engelhart, D., Hill, W.H., Furst, E.J. and Krathwohl, D.R. (1956) *Taxonomy of Educational Objectives: The Classification of Educational Goals*. Boston: Allyn and Bacon.

Brown, P.L. (2007) 'In the classroom, a new focus on quieting the mind', *New York Times*, 16 June. Available at http://www.nytimes.com/2007/06/16/us/16mindful.html (accessed 6/12/16).

Bruni, F. (2016) 'Turning the tide', *New York Times*. Available at https://www.nytimes.com/2016/01/20/opinion/rethinking-college-admissions.html (accessed 25/1/2017).

Burns, T. (2016) Educare. Available at www.timburnseducare.com/ (accessed 6/12/16).

Callard, F. and Margulies, D. (2011) 'The subject at rest: novel conceptualizations of self and brain from cognitive neuroscience's study of the "resting state"', *Subjectivity*, 4(3): 227–57. Available at http://link.springer.com/article/10.1057/sub.2011.11 (accessed 6/12/16).

Council in Schools (2010) 'The Ojai Foundation', 18 November. Available at www.youtube.com/watch?v=fKSh73dO49s (accessed 6/12/16).

Cozolino, L. (2013) *The Social Neuroscience of Education: Optimizing Attachment and Learning in the Classroom*. New York: Norton.

Dakin, N. (September 2016) Available at https://www.theyworkforyou.com/whall/?id=2016-09-06b.111.1 (accessed 25/1/2017).

Davidson, R. (2016) 'The four keys to well-being', *Greater Good*, 21 March. Available at http://greatergood.berkeley.edu/article/item/the_four_keys_to_well_being (accessed 6/12/16).

de Bruin, E.I., Blom, R., Smit, F.M.A., van Steensel, F.J.A. and Bogels, S.M. (2015) 'MYmind: mindfulness training for youngsters with autism spectrum disorders and their parents', *Autism*, 19(8): 906-914. Available at http://aut.sagepub.com/content/19/8/906 (accessed 6/12/16).

Dewey, J. (1897) 'My pedagogic creed', *School Journal*, 54 (January): 77-80. Available at http://dewey.pragmatism.org/creed.htm (accessed 6/12/16).

Diamond, D.M., Campbell, A.M., Park, C.R., Halonen, J. and Zoladz, P.R. (2007) 'The Temporal Dynamics Model of Emotional Memory Processing: A Synthesis on the Neurobiological Basis of Stress-Induced Amnesia, Flashbulb and Traumatic Memories, and the Yerkes-Dodson Law', *Neural Plasticity*, vol. 2007, Article ID 60803, 2007. doi:10.1155/2007/60803.

Dobkin, P. and Hutchinson, T. (2013) 'Teaching mindfulness in medical school: where are we now and where are we going?', *Medical Education*, 47: 768-79. Available at www.mcgill.ca/wholepersoncare/files/wholepersoncare/teaching_mindfulness.pdf (accessed 6/12/16).

Durlak, J.A., Weissberg, R.P., Dymnicki, A.B., Taylor, R.D. and Schellinger, K.B. (2011) 'The impact of enhancing SEL, A meta-analysis of school-based universal interventions', *Child Development*, 82(1): 405-432. Available at http://static1.squarespace.com/static/513f79f9e4b05ce7b70e9673/t/52e9d8e6e4b001f5c1f6c27d/1391057126694/meta-analysis-child-development.pdf (accessed 6/12/16).

Dweck, C. (2007) *Mindset: The New Psychology of Success*. New York: Ballantine.

Elbert, T., Pantev, C., Wienbruch, C., Rockstroh, B. and Taub, E. (1995) 'Increased cortical representation of the fingers of the left hand in string players', *Science*, New Series, 270(5234): 305-7. Available at www.ncbi.nlm.nih.gov/pubmed/7569982 (accessed 6/12/16).

Elias, M. and Zins, J.E. (1997) *Promoting Social and Emotional Learning: Guidelines for Educators*. Alexandria, VA: ASCD.

Farb, N., Segal, Z.V., Mayberg, H., Bean, J., McKeon, D., Fatima, Z. and Anderson, A. (2007) 'Attending to the present: mindfulness meditation reveals distinct neural modes of self-reference', *Social Cognitive and Affective Neuroscience*, 2(4): 313-22. Available at www.ncbi.nlm.nih.gov/pubmed/18985137 (accessed 6/12/16).

Feinberg, C. (2013) 'The placebo phenomenon', *Harvard Magazine*, January–February. Available at http://harvardmagazine.com/2013/01/the-placebo-phenomenon (accessed 6/12/16).

Felver, J.C., Celis-de Hoyos, C.E., Tezanos, K. and Singh, N.N. (2015) 'A systematic review of mindfulness-based interventions for youth in school settings', *Mindfulness*, 7(1). Available at www.researchgate.net/publication/273349460_A_Systematic_Review_of_Mindfulness-Based_Interventions_for_Youth_in_School_Settings (accessed 6/12/16).

Fielding, M. (2005) 'Putting hands around the flame: reclaiming the radical tradition in state education', *FORUM*, 47(2): 61-70. Available at www.wwwords.co.uk/rss/abstract.asp?j=forum&aid=2555 (accessed 6/12/16).

Gallagher, R.P. (2015) 'National Survey of College Counseling Centers 2014'. Available at http://0201.nccdn.net/1_2/000/000/088/0b2/NCCCS2014_v2.pdf (accessed 25/1/17).

Ginott, H. (1994 [1972]) *Teacher and Child: A Book for Parents and Teachers*. New York: Simon & Schuster.

Goldsmith, S.K., Pellmar, T.C., Kleinman, A.M. and Bunney, W.E. (eds) (2002) *Reducing Suicide: A National Imperative*, Committee on Pathophysiology and Prevention of Adolescent and Adult Suicide. Washington, D.C.: National Academies Press. Available at www.nap.edu/read/10398/chapter/1#ii (accessed 6/12/16).

Goleman, D. (1995) *Emotional Intelligence: Why It Can Matter More Than IQ*. New York: Bantam.

Goleman, D. (2013) *Focus: The Hidden Driver of Excellence*. New York: HarperCollins.

Goleman, D. and Senge, P. (2014) *Triple Focus: A New Approach to Education* (Kindle edn). Florence, MA: More than Sound.

Gunaratana, B. (2011) *Mindfulness in Plain English*. Somerville, MA: Wisdom.

Halevi, Y. (2002) 'Introspection as a prerequisite for peace', *New York Times*, 7 September. Available at www.nytimes.com/2002/09/07/opinion/introspection-as-a-prerequisite-for-peace.html (accessed 6/12/16).

Halliwell, E. (2014) 'Can mindfulness transform politics?', *Mindful*, 23 May. Available at www.mindful.org/can-mindfulness-transform-politics-2/ (accessed 6/12/16).

Harari, Y.N. (2014) *Sapiens: A Brief History of Humankind*. New York: Harper Collins.

Harvard Graduate School (2014) 'The children we mean to raise'. Available at http://mcc.gse.harvard.edu/the-children-we-mean-to-raise (accessed 6/12/16).

Harvard Graduate School (2015) 'Harvard turning the tide: inspiring concern for others and the common good through college admissions'. Available at http://mcc.gse.harvard.edu/files/gse-mcc/files/20160120_mcc_ttt_execsummary_interactive.pdf?m=1453303460 (accessed 6/12/16).

Hawley, D. (2016) 'Investigating stress in the DP', *IB World*, Issue 73. Available at https://issuu.com/internationalbaccalaureate/docs/ibo_eng_mar16_digi-mag4mb (accessed 6/12/16).

Helliwell, J., Layard, R. and Sachs, J. (eds) (2015) *World Happiness Report 2015*. New York: Sustainable Development Solutions Network. Available at http://worldhappiness.report/wp-content/uploads/sites/2/2015/04/WHR15.pdf (accessed 6/12/16).

Hennelly, S. (2010) 'The immediate and sustained effects of the .b mindfulness programme on adolescents' social and emotional well-being and academic functioning', Thesis submitted for Master of Research in Psychology, Oxford Brookes University.

Huppert, F.A. and So, T.T.C. (2011) Soc Indic Res. 110: 837. First available online 15 December 2011, DOI: 10.1007/S11205-011-9966-7.

Huxter, M. (2016) *Healing the Heart and Mind with Mindfulness*. London: Routledge.

Ingersoll, R. and Stuckey, D. (2014) 'Seven Trends: The Transformation of the Teaching Force', CPRE Report (RR#-80). Philadelphia: Consortium for Policy Research in Education, University of Pennsylvania.

James, W. (1890) *The Principles of Psychology*, Vols 1 and 2. New York: Holt.

Jennings, P. (2015) *Mindfulness for Teachers: Simple Skills for Peace and Productivity in the Classroom*. New York: Norton.

Jennings, P., Brown, J., Frank, J. Doyle, S., Oh, Y., Tanler, R., Rasheed, D., DeWeese, A., DeMauro, A., Cham, H., Greenberg, M. (2015) 'Promoting teachers' social and emotional competence and classroom quality: a randomized controlled trial of the CARE for Teachers professional development program', draft submission EDU-2015-1078R2, *Journal of Educational Psychology*.

Jensen, E., Bengaard Skibsted, E. and Christensen Vedsgaard, M. (2015) 'Educating teachers focusing on the development of reflective and relational competences', *Educational Research for Policy and Practice*, 14: 201. Available at http://link.springer.com/article/10.1007/s10671-015-9185-0 (accessed 25/1/17).

Johnson, D.C., Thom, N.J., Stanley, E.A., Haase, L., Simmons, A.N., Shih, P.B., Thompson, W.K., Potterat, E.G., Minor, T.R. and Paulus, M.P. (2014) 'Modifying resilience mechanisms in at-risk individuals: a controlled study of mindfulness training in marines preparing for deployment', *American Journal of Psychiatry*, 171(8): 844–53. Available at www.ncbi.nlm.nih.gov/pubmed/24832476 (accessed 6/12/16).

Kabat-Zinn, J. (1991) *Full Catastrophe Living: How to Cope with Stress, Pain and Illness using Mindfulness Meditation*. London: Piatkus.

Kabat-Zinn, J. (2013) 'Mindfulness in education'. Available at www.youtube.com/watch?v=Qm-qnkclUyE (accessed 6/12/16).

Kaiser-Greenland, S. (2010) *The Mindful Child: How to Help Your Kids Manage Stress, Become Happier, Kinder and More Compassionate*. New York: Free Press.

Kallapiran, K., Koo, S., Kirubakaran, R. and Hancock, K. (2015) 'Effectiveness of mindfulness in improving mental health symptoms of children and adolescents: a meta-analysis', *Child and Adolescent Mental Health*, 20(4): 182–94. Available at http://onlinelibrary.wiley.com/doi/10.1111/camh.12113/full (accessed 6/12/16).

Kemeny, M.E., Foltz, C., Cavanagh, J.F., Cullen, M., Giese-Davis, J., Jennings, P., Rosenberg, E.L., Gillath, O., Shaver, P.R., Wallace, B.A. and Ekman, P. (2011) 'Contemplative/emotion training reduces negative emotional behavior and promotes prosocial responses', *Emotion*, 12(2): 338–50. Available at www.paulekman.com/wp-content/uploads/2013/07/Contemplative-emotion-training-reduces-negative-emotional-behavior-and-promotes-prosocial-responses.pdf (accessed 6/12/16).

Kessler, R. (2000) *The Soul of Education: Helping Students Find Connection, Compassion and Character at School*. Alexandria, VA: ASCD.

Killingsworth, M.A. and Gilbert, D.T. (2010) 'A wandering mind is an unhappy mind', *Science*, 330(6006): 932. Available at http://science.sciencemag.org/content/330/6006/932.full (accessed 6/12/16).

Kornfield, J. (1993) *A Path with Heart: The Classic Guide Through the Perils and Promises of Spiritual Life*. New York: Bantam.

Kuyken, W., Weare, K., Ukoumunne, O., Vicary, R., Moton, N., Burnett, R., Cullen, C., Hennelly, S. and Huppert, F. (2013) 'Effectiveness of the Mindfulness in Schools Programme: non-randomised controlled feasibility study', *British Journal of Psychiatry*, 203(2): 126–31. Available at http://bjp.rcpsych.org/content/203/2/126.full.pdf+html (accessed 6/12/16).

Kyriacou, C. (2001b) 'Teacher stress: directions for future research', *Educational Review*, 53: 28–35.

Lantieri, L. (2008) *Building Emotional Intelligence*. Boulder, CO: Sounds True.

Lau, H. and Rosenthal, D. (2011) 'Empirical support for higher-order theories of conscious awareness', *Trends in Cognitive Sciences*, 15(8): 365–73. Available at http://neurocognitiva.org/wp-content/uploads/2014/04/Lau-2011-Empirical-support-for-higher-order-theories-of-conscious-awareness.pdf (accessed 6/12/16).

Lueke, A. and Gibson, B. (2014) Mindfulness meditation reduces implicit age and race bias: The role of reduced automaticity of responding. *Social Psychological and Personality Science SAGE Journals*. http://journals.sagepub.com/doi/abs/10.1177/1948550614559651 (accessed 5/2/2017).

Magee, R. (2015) How mindfulness can defeat racial bias. *The Greater Good, Science of a Meaningful Life*. http://greatergood.berkeley.edu/article/item/how_mindfulness_can_defeat_racial_bias (accessed 5/2/2017).

Maguire, E.A., Woollett, K. and Spiers, H.J. (2006) 'London taxi drivers and bus drivers: a structural MRI and neuropsychological analysis', *Hippocampus*, 16: 1091–1101. Available at www.ucl.ac.uk/spierslab/Maguire2006Hippocampus (accessed 6/12/16).

Marturano, J. (2014) *Finding the Space to Lead: A Practical Guide to Mindful Leadership*. New York: Bloomsbury.

Marzano, R.J. and Pickering, D.J. with Heflebower, T. (2011) *The Highly Engaged Classroom*. Bloomington, IN: Marzano Research Laboratory, pp. 5–7.

Massachusetts General Hospital (2011) 'Mindfulness meditation training changes brain structure in 8 weeks', *News Release*, 2 January. Available at www.massgeneral.org/news/pressrelease.aspx?id=1329 (accessed 6/12/16).

Mental Health Foundation (2015) 'Fundamental facts about mental health'. Available at www.mentalhealth.org.uk/sites/default/files/fundamental-facts-15.pdf (accessed 6/12/16).

Microsoft Canada (2015) 'Attention spans', *Consumer Insights*. Available at http://docplayer. net/13720026-Microsoft-attention-spans-spring-2015-msadvertisingca-msftattnspans-attention-spans-consumer-insights-microsoft-canada.html (accessed 24/1/17).

Mindfulness All-Party Parliamentary Group (MAPPG) (2015) *Mindful Nation UK*. London: The Mindfulness Initiative. Available at http://themindfulnessinitiative.org.uk/images/reports/Mindfulness-APPG-Report_Mindful-Nation-UK_Oct2015.pdf (accessed 13/12/16).

Moffitt, T.E., Arseneault, L., Belsky, D., Dickson, N., Hancox, R.J., Harrington, H.L., Houts, R., Poulton, R., Roberts, W., Ross, S., Sears, M.R., Thomson, W.M. and Caspi, A. 'A gradient of childhood self-control predicts health, wealth, and public safety', PNAS, 2011, 108 (7): 2693-2698; published ahead of print January 24, 2011. doi:10.1073/pnas.1010076108

Murphy, M. and Fonagy, P. (2012) 'Chapter 10: Mental health problems in children and young people', from Annual Report of the Chief Medical Officer, *Our Children Deserve Better: Prevention Pays*. Available at www.gov.uk/government/uploads/system/uploads/attachment_data/file/252660/33571_2901304_CMO_Chapter_10.pdf (accessed 6/12/16).

NASUWT (2016) 'Urgent action needed to reduce stress faced by teachers' Available at https://www.nasuwt.org.uk/article-listing/action-needed-to-reduce-stress-faced-by-teachers.html (accessed 26/1/17).

National Education Association (NEA) (2015) 'Research spotlight on recruiting and retaining highly qualified teachers'. Available at www.nea.org/tools/17054.htm (accessed 6/12/16).

National Institute for Health and Care Excellence (2009) 'Depression in adults: recognition and management', NICE guidelines CG90 last updated April 2016. Available at https://www.nice.org.uk/guidance/cg90 (accessed 26/1/17).

Parks, T. (2010) *Teach Us to Sit Still: A Sceptic's Search for Health and Healing*. London: Vintage.

Pattakos, A. (2004) *Prisoners of Our Thoughts*. Oakland, CA: Berrett-Koehler. Available at www.bkconnection.com/static/Prisoners-of-our-Thoughts-EXCERPT.pdf (accessed 6/12/16).

Patterson, K., Grenny, J., McMillan, R. and Switzler, A. (2002) *Crucial Conversations: Tools for Talking When Stakes are High*. New York: McGraw-Hill.

Patterson, K., Grenny, J., McMillan, R., Switzler, A. (2005) *Crucial Confrontations: Tools for Resolving Broken Promises, Violated Expectations and Bad Behaviour*. New York: McGraw-Hill.

Pbert, L., Madison, J.M., Druker, S, Olendzki, N., Magner, R., Reed, G., and Carmody, J. (2012) 'Effect of mindfulness training on asthma quality of life and lung function: a randomised controlled trial', *Thorax*, 67(9): 769-76. Available at www.ncbi.nlm.nih.gov/pmc/articles/PMC4181405 (accessed 6/12/16).

Pinger, L. and Flook, L. (2016) 'What if schools taught kindness?', The Greater Good Science Centre, University of California, Berkeley, CA. Available at http://greatergood.berkeley.edu/article/item/what_if_schools_taught_kindness (accessed 13/12/16).

Postman, N. (1995) *The End of Education: Redefining the Value of School*. New York: Vintage.

Powell, K. and Kusuma-Powell, O. (2010) *Becoming an Emotionally Intelligent Teacher*. London: Corwin.

Powell, W. and Kusuma-Powell, O. (2013) The OIQ Factor: Raising Your School's Organizational Intelligence. Woodbridge: John Catt Educational.

Rechstaffen, D. (2014) *The Way of Mindful Education: Cultivating Well-being in Teachers and Students*. New York: Norton.

Research Autism (2016) 'Mindfulness and autism publications'. Available at http://researchautism.net/autism-interventions/types/psychological-interventions/cognitive-and-behavioural-therapies/mindfulness-training-and-autism/mindfulness-and-autism-publications (accessed 6/12/16).

Robinson, K. (2010) 'Changing education paradigms'. Available at www.ted.com/talks/ken_robinson_changing_education_paradigms (accessed 6/12/16).

Rock, D. (2009) 'The neuroscience of mindfulness', *Psychology Today*, 11 October. Available at www.psychologytoday.com/blog/your-brain-work/200910/the-neuroscience-mindfulness (accessed 6/12/16).

Rodenburg, P. (2009) *Presence: How to Use Positive Energy for Success in Every Situation*. London: Penguin.

Ryan, T. (2012) *A Mindful Nation: How a Simple Practice Can Help Us Reduce Stress, Improve Performance and Recapture the American Spirit*. Carlsbad, CA: Hay House.

Saltzman, A. (2014) *A Still Quiet Place: A Mindfulness Program for Teaching Children and Adolescents to Ease Stress and Difficult Emotions*. Oakland, CA: New Harbinger.

Sanger, K. and Dorjee, D. (2016) 'Mindfulness training with adolescents enhances metacognition and the inhibition of irrelevant stimuli: evidence from event-related brain potentials', *Trends in Neuroscience and Education*, 5(1): 1–11. Available at www.sciencedirect.com/science/article/pii/S2211949316300011 (accessed 6/12/16).

Sapolsky, R. (2004) *Why Zebras Don't Get Ulcers*. New York: Holt.

Saron, C. (2013) 'Chapter 19: The Shamatha Project Adventure: a personal account of an ambitious meditation study and its first result', in *Compassion – Bridging Practice and Science*. Munich: Max Planck Society. Available at www.compassion-training.org/en/online/files/assets/basic-html/page345.html (accessed 6/12/16).

Scelfo, J. (2015) 'Teaching peace in elementary school', *New York Times*, 14 November. Available at www.nytimes.com/2015/11/15/sunday-review/teaching-peace-in-elementary-school.html?_r=2 (accessed 6/12/16).

Schank, R. and Cleave, J. (1995) 'Natural learning, natural teaching: changing human memory', in H. Morowitz and J.L. Singer (eds), *The Mind, the Brain, and Complex Adaptive Systems*. Reading, MA: Addison-Wesley. Available at https://searchworks.stanford.edu/view/2996709 (accessed 6/12/16).

Schoeberlein, D. (2009) *Mindful Teaching and Teaching Mindfulness: A Guide for Anyone who Teaches Anything*. Somerville, MA: Wisdom.

Schonert-Reichl, K.A., Oberlee, E., Lawlor, M.S., Abbott, D., Thomson, K. and Diamond, D. (2015) 'Enhancing cognitive and social-emotional development through a simple-to-administer mindfulness-based school program for elementary school children: a randomized controlled trial', *Developmental Psychology*, 51(1): 52–66. Available at www.ncbi.nlm.nih.gov/pmc/articles/PMC4323355/ (accessed 6/12/16).

Seligman, M. (2011) *Flourish: A Visionary New Understanding of Happiness and Well-being*. New York: Free Press.

Senge, P. (1990) *The Fifth Discipline: The Art and Practice of the Learning Organization*. London: Random House.

Senge, P., Cambron-McCabe, N. Lucas, T., Smith, B., Dutton, J. and Kleiner, A. (2000) *Schools That Learn: A Fifth Discipline Fieldbook for Educators, Parents, and Everyone Who Cares About Education*. London: Nicholas Brealey.

Srinivasan, M. (2014) *Teach, Breathe, Learn: Mindfulness In and Out of the Classroom*. Berkely, CA: Parallax.

Stone, J. (2015) 'Over focus on exams causing mental health problems and self-harm among pupils, study finds', *Independent*, 6 July. Available at www.independent.co.uk/news/uk/politics/over-focus-on-exams-causing-mental-health-problems-and-self-harm-among-pupils-study-finds-10368815.html (accessed 6/12/16).

Teasdale, J.D., Segal, Z.V., Williams, J.M., Ridgeway, V.A., Soulsby, J.M. and Lau, M.A. (2000) 'Prevention of relapse/recurrence in major depression by mindfulness-based cognitive therapy', *Journal of Consulting and Clinical Psychology*, 68(4): 615–23.

Available at www.radboudcentrumvoormindfulness.nl/media/Artikelen/Teasdale2000.pdf (accessed 6/12/16).

Twenge, J. (2000) 'Age of anxiety? Birth cohort changes in anxiety and neuroticism 1952-1993', *Journal of Personality and Social Psychology*, 79(6): 1007-21. Available at www.apa.org/pubs/journals/releases/psp7961007.pdf (accessed 6/12/16).

Vickery, C. and Dorjee, D. (2016) 'Mindfulness training in primary schools decreases negative affect and increases meta-cognition in children', *Frontiers in Psychology*, 12 January. Available at http://journal.frontiersin.org/article/10.3389/fpsyg.2015.02025/full (accessed 6/12/16).

Wake Forest Baptist Medical Center (2015) 'Mindfulness meditation trumps placebo in pain reduction.' *ScienceDaily*, 10 November 2015. Available at: https://www.sciencedaily.com/releases/2015/11/151110171600.htm (accessed 14/03/17).

Watts, T. (2014) 'George Mason's "Well-Being University" (extended cut)', *Vimeo*. Available at https://vimeo.com/114250339 (accessed 6/12/16).

Weare, K. (2013) 'Developing mindfulness with children and young people: a review of the evidence and policy context', *Journal of Children's Services*, 8(2): 141-53. Available at https://mindfulnessinschools.org/wp-content/uploads/2013/03/children-and-mindfulness-journal-of-childrens-services-weare.pdf (accessed 6/12/16).

Weare, K. (2014) 'Evidence for mindfulness: impacts on the wellbeing and performance of school staff', Mindfulness in Schools Project, University of Exeter. Available at https://mindfulnessinschools.org/wp-content/uploads/2014/10/Evidence-for-Mindfulness-Impact-on-school-staff.pdf (accessed 6/12/16).

Weaver, L. and Wilding, M. (2013) *The Five Dimensions of Engaged Teaching: A Practical Guide for Educators*. Bloomington, IN: Solution Tree Press.

Willard, C. (2016) *Growing Up Mindful: Essential Practices to Help Children, Teens, and Families Find Balance, Calm, and Resilience*. Boulder, CO: Sounds True.

Williams, J.M.G. (2010) 'Mindfulness and psychological process', *Emotion*, 10(1): 1-7. Available at www.oxfordmindfulness.org/dev/uploads/Williams-2010-Mindfulness-and-psychological-process.pdf (accessed 6/12/16).

Williams, J.M., Barnhofer, T., Crane, C., Duggan, D.S., Shah, D., Brennan, K., Krusche, A., Crane, R., Eames, C., Jones, M., Radford, S. and Russell, I.T. (2012) 'Pre-adult onset and patterns of suicidality in patients with a history of recurrent depression', *Journal of Affective Disorders*, 138(1-2): 173-9. Available at www.bangor.ac.uk/mindfulness/documents/earlyonsetdepression.pdf (accessed 6/12/16).

Williams, M. and Penman, D. (2011) *Mindfulness: A Practical Guide to Finding Peace in a Frantic World*. London: Piatkus.

Williams, M., Teasdale, J., Segal, Z. and Kabat-Zinn, J. (2007) *The Mindful Way Through Depression: Freeing Yourself from Chronic Unhappiness*. New York: Guilford Press.

World Health Organization (WHO) (2012) 'Depression: A Global Crisis - World Mental Health Day, October 10 2012'. Available at www.who.int/mental_health/management/depression/wfmh_paper_depression_wmhd_2012.pdf (accessed 6/12/16).

World Health Organization (WHO) (2016) 'Adolescents: health risks and solutions', Fact Sheet 345. Available at www.who.int/mediacentre/factsheets/fs345/en/ (accessed 6/12/16).

Yerkes, R.M. and Dodson, J.D. (1908) 'The relation of strength of stimulus to rapidity of habit-formation', *Journal of Comparative Neurology and Psychology*, 18: 459-82.

Zeidan, F., Emerson N.M., Farris, S.R., Ray, J.N., Jung, Y., McHaffie, J.G. and Coghill, R.C. (2015) 'Mindfulness meditation-based pain relief employs different neural mechanisms than placebo and sham mindfulness meditation-induced analgesia', *Journal of Neuroscience*, 35(46): 15307-325. Available at www.ncbi.nlm.nih.gov/pubmed/26586819 (accessed 6/12/16).

Index